Maharajas' Palaces

Portrait of the Maharaja of Kapurthala, Jagatjit Singh,
who wrote his diary in French.

Maharajas' Palaces

European style in Imperial India

Photographs
Anne Garde

Text
Sylvie Raulet

Foreword
Laure Vernière

The Vendome Press

© 1996 Éditions Hazan, Paris

The Vendome Press
1370 Avenue of the Americas
Suite 2003
New York, NY 10019

Distributed in
the U.S.A. and Canada by
Rizzoli International Publications
through St. Martin's Press
175 Fifth Avenue
New York, NY 10010

Library of Congress Cataloging-in-Publication Data
Raulet, Sylvie.
    Majarajas' palaces / by Sylvie Raulet and Laure Vernière;
photographs by Anne Garde.
        p. cm.
    Includes bibliographical references.
    ISBN 0-86565-989-3
    1. Palaces--India. 2. Architecture--India--European influences.
3. India--Kings and rulers--Homes and haunts. I. Vernière, Laure,
1941-   . II. Title.
NA1501,R36 1997
728.8'2'0954--dc21   97-5250
                             CIP

ISBN: 0-86565-989-3

English translation © 1997 Philip Wilson Publishers Ltd and The Vendome Press

Translation from French by
Judith Hayward

English edition edited by
Cherry Lewis

Colour separation by
Colourscan, Paris

Printing by
Artegrafica, Verona

Printed in Italy

CONTENTS

The old fort of Morvi, the iron gates of the zenana.

In 1902 the Maharaja of Kapurthala commissioned a replica of the palace of Versailles to be built on the Punjab plains. His love affair with France was all embracing: the one hundred apartments of the new palace were filled with Sèvres porcelain, Gobelins tapestries and Aubusson carpets; the Maharaja spoke fluent French, and wrote his diary in that language.

He was not alone. The Maharaja of Baroda had an English majordomo, a French cook, an Italian chauffeur, ordered his linen from Belfast and his porcelain from Bond Street. From the late nineteenth to the early twentieth century, Indian princes, nawabs, rajas, and maharajas, as well as wealthy Indian merchants, wearing turbans, but otherwise dressed in European clothes, were constantly to be found in the most exclusive shops in London and Paris, buying Louis XV furniture, Meissen porcelain and Venetian glass, commissioning custom-built Rolls Royces and resetting their priceless jewellery à la Art Deco. They employed European interior designers, architects and landscape gardeners, sent their children to school and university in the West, and sometimes married European wives.

Why this fascination for all things European? No doubt the association with India of European traders since the 1500s, together with the British government of India for almost one hundred years from 1857, were the overriding influences on the desire to copy and imitate. Yet it is an ironic twist of cultural fashion that the West, which for so long had admired, copied and purchased the decorative arts of the Indian subcontinent should, in this strange case of role reversal, find its own artistic styles and manufactured wares irresistible to these wealthy princes.

The 'European taste' in maharajas' palaces produced some bizarre arrangements, but it also saw exciting and imaginative work. The architecture of Lutyens and Baker in New Delhi is well known; the interior decoration of the Maharaja of Indore's palace was influenced by the distinguished German designer Muthesius and includes furniture by Le Corbusier; and as early as the mid-seventeenth century European craftsmen were consulted and worked on the Taj Mahal.

Always impressive, sometimes overwhelming, never dull, these magnificent colour images of the ornamentation and interior decoration of great princely palaces taken by Anne Garde, and described by Sylvie Raulet, take us into a world where we see cross-cultural art at its most exciting and extravagant.

Foreword

The story of this book begins in Aquitaine when Anne Garde, still a child at the time, discovered a bottle of a great wine in a Bordeaux wine store with the mysterious label: 'Château-Lafite 1875. Return from India. Dispatched aboard the steamship Précurseur *which sailed from Bordeaux on 31 October 1878 for Bombay and Madras, returned to Bordeaux on 22 April 1879.'* Even if there were other bottles that did not come back (if we are to believe the annals of Château Cos d'Estournel whose entire harvest was destined for India from 1830 to 1850), wine was used as ballast for ships setting off on the spice trade, and it came back to the port of origin improved, prematurely aged by its travels. Anne Garde was often to think of that symbolic bottle when this strange photographic adventure led her to commute frequently between Paris and India - searching for the traces and evidence of the influence of Europe on architecture, the decorative arts and the Indian way of life. The present-day vestiges of that influence on the formidable democracy that India has become since achieving Independence in 1947 are the subject of this book.

That story grew in scope in the spring of 1983 when memories were revived by The Music Room, *a Bengali film first seen by French cinema-lovers in the 1960s. Satyajit Ray, the great master of cinema from Calcutta, had shot the film not far from Murshidabad, the former capital of the Nawabs of Bengal, who in the eighteenth century had been allies of the French against the East India Company (Britain's great commercial empire in India). The alliance ended with Robert Clive's victory over Nawab Suraj ud Daula at the Battle of Plassey in 1757.*

Here the name of Claude Martin makes an appearance: the son of a modest Lyonnais silk merchant, he started life as a simple French soldier and went on to became captain, colonel and ultimately general in the British Army, eventually becoming the confidant of Nawab Asaf ud Daula of Lucknow, negotiating between the Moslem king and the East India Company. Martin, also a builder and humanist, was one of those exceptional adventurers who knew how to teach the Indian princes to appreciate things European.

At roughly the same time, Tippoo Sultan (also known as Tippoo Sahib) died a hero's death on 4 May 1799 at the storming of Seringapatam pursuing his struggle against the British. Tippoo cut a romantic figure as sultan at the court of Mysore, and like his father - the great adventurer Haidar Ali - before him he retained close contacts with the French, sending an embassy to the court of Versailles in 1788 and even becoming a 'citizen of the French Revolution' a few years later! Tippoo the Tiger had summoned French craftsmen to Mysore during his reign, again following his father's example, and it was one of these who made the mechanism for the famous musical tiger. This strange wooden automaton, which snarls as it attacks a British enemy, has long been an object of wonder at the Victoria and Albert Museum, and *still fascinates visitors to the recently created Nehru Gallery: another strange quirk of history in this unique, sometimes cruel saga of Europe's relations with India.*

So what is the legacy of that touching, slightly ludicrous attraction for all things European, which no doubt had its origin in the complex relationships between Europe and India, and Indians and westerners? It is a well-known fact that from the time the Portuguese first set foot in India in the sixteenth century people went there with self-interested aims: to convert, to do business, and to take possession of and, under specious pretexts, even usurp territory . But once there, they were overcome with awe: India was remote, barbaric, fantastic, huge and unreal, and this is how it is described to us in travellers' tales - for instance, those of Bernier, Tavernier, Manucci or Austin of Bordeaux, a goldsmith working on the Taj Mahal.

Later on, daily life 'with the English' - to turn Pierre Loti's title L'Inde (sans les Anglais) *on its head - led to the 'poor' taste shown by these princes and high-caste intellectuals for European exoticism; educated at Cambridge or Oxford, they juggled Shakespeare and the* Ramayana *and 'did business' on occasion with Danish, Portuguese, French or Dutch diplomats, soldiers and missionaries. At the same time, when there was a great deal of trade between India and Europe, the enormously rich merchants - the Marwaris in Calcutta or the Parsees in Bombay - also furnished their luxurious residences in the European style. Anything and everything could be bought in Calcutta, then the capital of the Raj: grand pianos, Swiss clocks, furniture from Lazarus, crystal chandeliers from Bohemia, Italianate statues and erotic pictures, Limoges china and Baccarat cut glass.*

But there was nonetheless a certain ambiguity about this taste for Europe, for it first and foremost expressed a desire to take on 'the White Man's burden', to use Kipling's controversial expression; power was ultimately slipping out of the hands of the Indian elite which did not have the freedom of the city in 'white' Calcutta, the façade of which echoed that of Liverpool or Bordeaux.

The fascination for Europe was thus often an elaborate Indian way of fitting in with the western style and responding to its 'exotic' way of living by the more artful means of imitation. The sumptuous Louis XV drawing-room with its dark, stiff furniture was often just a formal setting for receiving foreign guests with conventional pomp. It concealed a reverse side: a music room where comfortable cushions of embroidered silk replaced ivory and crystal seats, and elegant miniatures derided the imposing oil portraits at the front of the stage. In the wings an oriental boudoir shielded the ladies of the zenana, eating the very sweet milk-based cardamon-flavoured sweetmeats, from indiscreet eyes.

In the 1920s the Cristalleries Baccarat agreed to part, for an astronomical sum, with the creation that had become their mascot, and which symbolized the entry of the City of Paris into the twentieth century. One of only two great crystal vessels with graceful gilt-bronze cherubs became the trophy of the Maharaja of Bikaner, who spent part of the year living in London and enjoyed visits to Paris. This treasure can now be found in the remote depths of Rajasthan: a feat of French craftsmanship has become a splendid, dusty hostage in the immense shuttered drawing-room of the Palace of Bikaner.

In the 1930s - and until Independence - artistic and intellectual contacts between Europe and the Indian subcontinent flourished, highlighted later by the unlikely but remarkable relationship between Lady Mountbatten and Pandit Nehru. Some palaces dating from this period are a marvellous expression of that amazing, albeit politically fragile 'renaissance'. Those times could be summed up as a 'twilight of the gods', where hope for change brought about by non-violent means led to the death of Gandhi and the final victory of India. These 'last-minute' palaces have miraculously overcome all the mockery and clumsiness of a crossbred and sometimes overworked art.

The best example of these is the Rashtrapati Bhavan, the government palace which is the spectacular culmination of imperial Delhi. This architectural scheme - the most ambitious in the history of British India - was completed in 1929 by Sir Edwin Lutyens and Sir Herbert Baker, the former the architect of the incomparable Viceroy's House, the latter of the Secretariat buildings. Seldom has 'official' architecture - the aim was for the scheme to be 'classical' in its mass, based on a geometrical vocabulary rejecting both the Indo-Saracenic and Hindu-Mogul traditions - so successfully integrated such powerful imagination and such intelligence in an oriental urban landscape. Forgetting disputes about schools and ideologies, there can be nothing more moving than the slow, orchestrated emergence of the pink dome of the central palace in the dip of the lower part of Raisina Hill as one walks up the majestic Rajpath. Today this palace, with its monumental columns built to the glory of the Raj, and concealing stone elephants and cobras in its gardens, is a triumphant symbol of the new Indian democracy, thus giving the lie to Georges Clémenceau who looked at imperial Delhi when it was under construction in 1920 and said: 'It will make a superb ruin. . .'

Once one gains access to some of these Indian drawing-rooms which attest to the fascination Indians felt for Europe, there is no option but to accept the fact that the spirits of Brancusi, Patrick Geddes, Pierre-Henri Roché, Marcel Duchamp, Mircea Eliade, Le Corbusier and Fritz Lang have long since deserted them. All that is then left is a kitsch Anglo-Indian décor, with the finest pieces having been sold off for a few rupees in prestigious European auction-rooms. The palace of Indore is an empty shell, while the strange furniture designed by Muthesius for his university friend, the Prince of Indore - the last ruler of the Holkar dynasty - can now be seen in Paris. The large 'Birds in Space' - one white marble, the other black - made by Brancusi between 1931 and 1936 for a scheme for a Temple of Deliverance at Indore, are in exile in Canberra Museum.

Today Indian connoisseurs travel around, but in earlier times princes often gave a helping hand to commercial agents who lacked any cultivation or stylistic discrimination. There are no great collections or objects that really stand out among the plentiful and whimsical décors, where an imitation Bernini or a false Michelangelo still look resplendent. This Italianate statuary, in imitation sometimes disorientating, merges into the oriental background. The unique charm of these interiors lies in the accumulation and unexpected juxtaposition of objects taken, sometimes haphazardly and unthinkingly, from the two major cultures.

From Rajasthan to Bengal one occasionally comes across pretty pseudo-Greek statues, a daub celebrating Romeo and Juliet or a modern-style lamp with a clumsy shade which all nod in the direction of Europe. But fortunately, along the way one also finds exuberant, original frescoes by Norblin - a Polish artist who fled from Nazism and ended his eventful career in the United States, a chandelier suggestive of Calder, Cubist blue-mirror furniture vibrant with magical crystal, a Venus smiling at a Gandhara Buddha, a graceful marble female figure poised to dive into an Art Deco swimming-pool. . .

But two instances are complete, unqualified successes: the Lutyens palace, a masterpiece of ceremonial architecture going beyond the norm and any compromises, and the new palace built by the Morvi family in the 1940s, a dazzling personal feat. Standing in the rather barren province of Gujarat on the edge of the Kutch desert, it is an authentic example of Indian inventiveness, suddenly reversing the usual European conformism and creating a third style. Its architecture is rigorously - almost militarily - pure, in the wake of the Modern Movement. Inside, forty or so rooms arranged on three floors - bedrooms, drawing-rooms, dining-rooms, games' rooms, libraries, bars and a swimming-pool - overlook two huge, simple courts, combining to create an architecture that cannot be categorized. Indian tradesmen and craftsmen working under Norblin's instructions managed to divert, revive, adapt and create a total Indian-style Art Deco, a new crossbreed where through some strange alchemy duplication has been transmuted into something original: the counterfeit has become the authentic, and make-believe has been metamorphosed into art.

Laure Vernière

I N 1498 THE PORTUGUESE, under the command of Vasco da Gama, were the first to set foot on Indian ground in search of new markets. They were joined soon after by the Dutch, Danish, English and French, all wishing primarily to get rich by establishing themselves and creating stable commercial relations with the local populations; they did not in fact have any ambitions towards territorial conquest. Thanks to the creation of the East India Company in 1600, a company accorded a guaranteed monopoly by Queen Elizabeth I, the English soon secured the lion's share of any trading; from the eighteenth century British merchants exported their goods to Calcutta, then the capital of India. However, following the Indian Mutiny in 1857, a terrible rebellion by the Sepoys, the powers held by the Company were transferred to the British Crown: the colonizing process was under way.

Siddhpur is a good example of Europe's influence on the rich dynasties of Indian merchants. While most Moslems coming from the north destroyed towns and villages on their way, seeing them as transgressing the principles of Islam, in the early eighteenth century, the Boras occupied Siddhpur by peaceful means. Forced to flee Ahmedabad and the fanaticism of Aurangzeb, a Mogul king with Moslem beliefs who found their tolerance unbearable, the Boras regarded themselves as exiles. Once the British had built a railway network, the Boras were able to cross frontiers, establishing very profitable trading relations with Ethiopia, Aden, Burma and Siam. When they had acquired their wealth, these travelling merchants did not forget Siddhpur, the only fixed point in their nomadic lives: at the end of the nineteenth century, wanting to leave their mark on this remote community and design a new town, they turned to a British architect. Built to a strict grid plan, the new town marked a complete break with the traditional lack of town-planning. The diversity and richness of the ornamentation on the façades, Victorian, Edwardian and Art Deco in style, come from the rivalry that still existed between the rich families: each family wanting to own the grandest and most striking house to reflect its wealth, had the family monogram and the name of the town where it had made its fortune carved on the façade.

Of all the courts of the moribund Mogul dynasty, the court of the kingdom of Oudh took the palm for cultural and artistic refinement. Shuja ud Daula, Nawab from 1753 to 1775, was certainly the first to break with the Persian-inspired way of life then prevailing in the kingdom and open his mind to European culture. The reputation of the French army was so high that after suffering a military defeat at Buxar, Shuja ud Daula decided to secure the services of one Colonel Gentil and other European officers. It was also at this time that he invited to his court the English portrait painter Tilly Kettle, who immortalized the ruling family. The huge fortune of his successor, Asaf ud Daula, maintained the large number of Europeans whom he summoned to his palace at Lucknow, the new capital of the kingdom: Colonel John Mordaunt, an English nobleman who commanded his bodyguard; the Frenchman General Claude Martin, a collector of objets d'art who was to build the Constantia palace in Lucknow; and the Swiss Colonel Polier, another art lover who contributed towards perfecting the Nawab's taste, at the same time selling him objects of variable quality. It can be assumed from contacts such as these that the Nawab evinced a lively curiosity towards western art; a room was set aside specially for his European collection of mirrors, crystal chandeliers and automata, then very fashionable in Europe.

This interest became a total fascination during the reigns of his successors, Ghazi ud Din Haidar (1814-1827) and Nasir ud Din Haidar (1827-1837). The former appointed a Scottish artist, Robert Home, as his official court painter, and both rulers went so far as to wear European-style clothes and receive their guests in a pavilion of neo-classical design.

There was one Indian ruler above all others whose fate was closely linked to France - Tippoo Sultan of Mysore. With the help of French army instructors, he stood up to the British for over thirty years. The three ambassadors he sent to the court of Louis XVI in 1788 brought back a Sèvres porcelain coffee service as a present from the king, and at the same time Tippoo collected European objets d'art, and employed French artists to design and make the furniture for his palace.

There were in fact two elite groups in India affected by western culture. The first were the nawabs and sultans who had invited European travellers to stay in their palaces ever since the Indian subcontinent had been 'discovered'. The second were the great merchants; after leaving their ancestral lands to establish trading relations between the East and the West, they were so attracted by the West that they built themselves residences in a European architectural style.

But it was in the second half of the nineteenth century, after the British had encouraged the maharajas to send their sons to Indian colleges which provided a perfect English-style education, that the European influence deepened. The sons then became perfect 'gentlemen', modelling their life style on that of the Europeans: they had their legendary jewels reset by European jewellers, travelled in magnificent limousines, eagerly played European sports, imported great Bordeaux wines and Évian water, and sent envoys to ransack London and Paris stores to furnish their huge palaces in the European style. Some - like the Maharaja of Indore who built himself an Art Deco palace - were so imbued with western culture that they even turned to European architects, among whom great figures from the Modern Movement feature, Le Corbusier to name one.

THE TAJ MAHAL AT AGRA

Regarded as one of the seven wonders of the world, the Taj Mahal was one of the first Indian buildings on which European craftsmen were employed. It was built between 1632 and 1648 at Agra, at that time the capital of the Mogul Empire, by the Mogul Emperor Shah Jahan to house the mortal remains of his adored wife, Mumtaz Mahal, who died giving birth to her fourteenth child. Very little is known about the genesis and building of the mausoleum, since the contemporary documents available and the accounts by travellers who visited India in the seventeenth century contradict one another. While we do not know who the architect entrusted with overall supervision of the work was, it is probable that several supervisory architects were employed to fulfil this magnificent commission: about 20,000 masons, quarrymen, marble masons and decorators worked on the project. We do know that Ustad Ahmad, assisted by his brother Ustad Hamid, is supposed to have drawn up the plans of the building; that a Turkish architect, a disciple of the great Sinan, the supreme architect and builder of the Ottoman Empire, was apparently consulted; that the Venetian Geronimo Veroneo is said to be the originator of the master drawing for the positioning of the building, in close conjunction with the configuration of the surrounding Mogul gardens; and that the Frenchman Augustin (or Austin) of Bordeaux was reputedly given the title of 'inventor of the arts'.

The decorative repertoire of the building links calligraphic work, geometric motifs and floral friezes inlaid in milk-white marble. While the use of floral motifs had been an essential part of the ornamental grammar of Mogul art since the seventeenth century, the floral iconography of the Taj Mahal draws its inspiration from western sources: in particular among the ornamentation we find flowers that grow neither in India nor, even on a wider scale, in the East. It is highly probably that botanical works and European herbals had reached the Mogul court via agents of the European trading companies or Jesuit missionaries.

The inlaying of semi-precious stones or *pietre dure* in marble and sandstone, a tradition handed down from the artistic heritage of Persia and Central Asia, brings Florentine work to mind. Writing about the Taj Mahal in the seventeenth century François Bernier, who spent some ten years in India and was received at the court of Emperor Aurangzeb, Shah Jahan's son, mentioned the Florentine 'commessi di pietre dure' in the following context: '. . .One sees only *yashm* or jade, only stones of the kind used to embellish the grand-duke's chapel in Florence, only jasper and several other types of rare, valuable stones, worked in a hundred ways, intermingled and set into the marbles covering the main walls. . .' (in *Voyages contenant la description des États du Grand Moghol, de l'Indoustan, du Royaume de Cachemire*, 1699). Moreover, it is recorded that Florentine *pietre dure* panels were sent to the Mogul court from Europe, and that the court asked eminent European artists to carry out such work.

AN ART DECO MODEL: THE MANIK BAGH PALACE AT INDORE

The palace at Indore, the most highly populated city in Madhya Pradesh which lies 500 kilometres north-east of Bombay, was commissioned by Yeswant Rao Holkar Bahadur, a young ruler educated by a British tutor and receptive to the western avant-garde. Henri-Pierre Roché, the author of the novel *Jules et Jim*, introduced him to modern art, especially to that of Brancusi and Duchamp. Initially the commission for a new royal residence had gone to a British architect but on his father's death, in May 1930, Yeswant Rao Holkar Bahadur stopped the

Desk designed by the Berlin architect Eckart Muthesius for the Art Deco palace of the Maharaja of Indore. Galerie Doria, Paris

work and approached the Berlin designer Eckart Muthesius who introduced him to the aesthetic ideas of Mackintosh and the rationalist theories of the Bauhaus.

Where the interior furnishing is concerned, we cannot fail to be impressed by the unerring choice in the artists approached: in the Maharaja's bedroom, a steel bed commissioned from Ruhlmann, a reclining steel chaise-longue upholstered in leo-pard skin designed in 1928 by Le Corbusier, carpets designed by Da Silva Bruhns, a bed-tester inlaid with glass and splinters of gilded mirror; in the library two red leather armchairs made in Berlin, with an ashtray and electric light switch built into the arm-rests. The Maharanee's dressing-table was ordered from Sognot & Alix, while in various parts of the palace there were pieces designed by Charlotte Perriand, light fittings by Perzel, fabrics by Hélène Henry and Rodier, furniture by Le Corbusier, and so on. Unfortunately this complete collection was dispersed in 1980 at a major sale organized by Sotheby's.

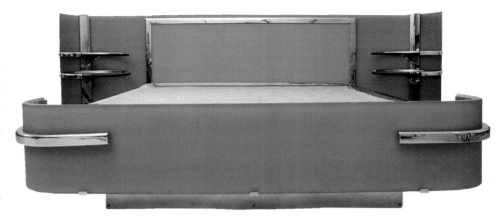

Bed forming part of the furnishings of the Art Deco palace of the Maharaja of Indore. Created by the Berlin architect Eckart Muthesius, whom the Maharaja commissioned to design the architecture and interior decoration of his palace. Galerie Doria, Paris

THE MODERN MOVEMENT IN PUBLIC BUILDINGS

In 1947, the year India was granted Independence and when partition took place, the Punjab was divided along an arbitrary demarcation line, giving rise to migration on a scale unprecedented in the history of mankind. As Lahore, the historic capital of the Punjab, became part of Pakistan, the Indian government decided to build a new town from scratch in the Indian sector - a decision indicative of the progressive spirit which activated Indians immediately following Independence - and to appoint Le Corbusier architectural adviser to the Punjab. Le Corbusier was asked to draw up plans for the town, a grid of avenues divided into about forty sectors. Chandigarh, built between 1951 and 1964, bears the stamp not only of Le Corbusier but also of the British architects Maxwell Fry and Jane Drew, as well as a team of Indian architects and town-planners. The three most spectacular buildings are all grouped in sector 1, lying beneath the foothills of the Himalayas: the Secretariat building, seat of the governments of the Punjab and Haryana, the Viddhan Sabha, housing the parliaments of both states, sporting a monumental portico supported by concrete columns, and the Supreme Court of Justice with a roof reminiscent of an umbrella turned inside out by a strong wind.

Ever since it was built, supporters and opponents of Chandigarh have unceasingly added fuel to the debate, the former noting the great boldness in the design combining modernist concepts and elements taken from traditional Indian architecture, while the latter condemn the questionable transplantation of western town-planning theories to Indian soil - and more specifically, the use of concrete which has been attacked by the monsoon rains.

As the undisputed master of the Modern Movement, Le Corbusier was approached to design the Millowners' Association building at Ahmedabad as well as a cultural centre and three private houses. Again at Ahmedabad, the American architect Louis Kahn designed the Indian Management Institute building, constructed between 1962 and 1972.

The resulting influence of Le Corbusier and followers of the Modern Movement on Indian architects was to prove patchy. However, among others mention should be made of B.V. Doshi, a former collaborator of Le Corbusier

The Capitol at Chandigarh, designed by Le Corbusier in the 1950s.

who designed the Tagore Hall and the Institute of Indology at Ahmedabad, Charles Correa and Uttam Jain; and of Raj Rewal, keen to combine the values of modern European architecture with a return to the basic principles of the Indian tradition, as seen in a number of schemes for the public sector in the Delhi area. While the various buildings designed by these architects reveal an undeniable western influence, they are also an attempt to reappropriate traditional Indian motifs in an original, inventive way, while avoiding pastiche: a tricky balancing act that most of the foremost Indian architects have been trying to achieve for almost half a century, not without success.

ARTISTS AND COLLECTORS

More than fifty years before the establishment of art schools - which would play a crucial role in spreading knowledge of European art - a spate of portrait painters and landscape artists from Europe had a profound influence on Indian artistic life and the ideas of artists and tastes of art lovers and collectors. Among the most influential were Tilly Kettle (1740-1786) whose paintings were very much admired by the Indian princes; Johann Zoffany (1733-1810) who lived in Calcutta from 1783 to 1789, but whose works were valued more by the European residents; William Hodges (1744-1799) who after a journey to India between 1781 and 1784 published a series of watercolour tinted engravings, including *Select Views in India* in 1786 and *Travels in India* in 1793; and Thomas Daniell (1749-1840) and his nephew William Daniell (1769-1837) who, after spending some time in Calcutta, travelled throughout the country and also published series of engravings such as *Views of Calcutta* (1786-1788) and *Oriental Scenery* (1808). The picturesque, exotic rural landscapes and architectural views - the favourite themes of all these artists - immortalized by the engravings delighted both affluent Indians and westerners wishing to take a memento of their time in India back to Europe. In turn, the enormous success of the engravings stimulated a proliferation of landscapes and architectural scenes executed by Indian artists, sometimes influenced by Europeans acting as their tutors. Native painters then adopted western aesthetic conventions, in particular where the treatment of shade or perspective were concerned. Art schools were established in Calcutta, Madras and Bombay in the 1850s, and in Lahore in 1875, and these set out to inculcate contemporary Victorian supposed 'good taste' into their students, but although a few Indian artists such as Raja Ravi Varma of Travancore achieved great renown, most had to be satisfied with acting as copyists of European works.

Exhibitions in India also played an important role in promulgating knowledge of the fine arts. The first exhibition to be held was organized in Calcutta in 1831-2 by British artists and a group of art-lovers known as the Brush Club. Paintings of Indian scenes by Hodges, Kettle, Zoffany, Chinnery and Beechey hung alongside paintings by Joshua Reynolds and Canaletto and copies of great seventeenth-century European masters like Guido Reni, Rubens and Van Dyck. Rich Bengalis such as Raja Ramanat Thakur (1801-1877), Jatindramohan Thakur (1831-1908) and Raja Rajendra Mullick became great collectors of western art, buying paintings by contemporary nineteenth-century artists, copies of canvases by great western masters hanging in museums in Europe - Raphael, Titian, Van Dyck, Guido Reni to name a few - and copies of Greek and Roman sculptures. Owning European works of art was regarded at the time by the great aristocratic and merchant families as the most dazzling outward symbol of their wealth.

While many works of art were imported from Europe, Calcutta had its own sales circuits; local sales were prompted by changes in collectors' tastes, fluctuations in wealth, or the dispersal of the paintings held at the Government Art Gallery at Calcutta in 1905.

Not until the beginning of the twentieth century did E.B. Havell, head of the Calcutta School of Art from 1896 to 1906, lead a national movement encouraging the study of Indian artistic traditions - long neglected because of the European tastes of rich Indian collectors - and supporting the development of a new indigenous style.

THE DECORATIVE ARTS

For centuries there was no furniture in Indian interiors: princes and humble people alike lived at floor level on carpets, mats and cushions. The only item of furniture in use was the chest where clothes were kept. It was not until the nineteenth century that the maharajas, inspired by the British way of life, altered the interior decoration of their palaces. No doubt the increasingly sedentary nature of their lives (wars between states were less frequent than before) was also a factor in their desire to have more comfortable homes.

As Rousselet noted in 1870 in *L'Inde des rajahs*, the influence of Europe on the way of life of rich Hindus was considerable: 'Their houses are magnificent and always contain such a quantity of furniture, *objets d'art*, mirrors and chandeliers that you would think you were in a shop. Generally these wonders are piled up indiscriminately; but it must be said that the owner regards them simply as a collection of valuable curiosities calculated to give visitors from the provinces an exalted idea of his position, while he himself as often as not is happy to use a nice Indian bedroom in a corner of his palace'.

The memoirs of Émile Guimet who travelled in India in the 1870s are no less eloquent. Writing about the Palace of Tanjore he asks: 'How can one describe all the curiosities in bad taste in this immense hall? Three ill-assorted grand pianos. On great tables there are crystal balls, artificial flowers under glass domes, wax fruit, birds made of spun glass and other *objets d'art*. A gilt swing-divan. Empire-style clocks: Ajax, Joan of Arc's companion-at-arms Dunois and other heroes whose speciality it is to tell the time, unless the clock has stopped, which it has. And then sentimental paintings inspired by the novels of Balzac with explanatory captions: "She becomes a great lady"; "She is in prison"; "She begs for the poor". Alongside enormous fantastic lanterns shaped like birds, with a woman's head and a gazelle's feet.' Thus knick-knacks and trinkets bought in Paris or London along with silver frames containing family photographs or signed portrait photographs of eminent Europeans were piled up in these palaces as in

Ali Baba's cave. For instance the Maharaja of Kutch displayed portraits of the French ministers of the Third Republic whom he had met in the 1920s at the League of Nations.

Indian princes were not the only ones to be infatuated with European goods - furniture, *objets d'art*, paintings - as a means of establishing their social status. The residences of the Bengali merchant aristocracy were also full of them; inside, as well as copies of Old Masters, there tended more particularly to be portraits by European painters working in India. As in Calcutta, so in Bombay, which in the nineteenth century had become India's major port with new industrial magnates living in great style in the smart districts of the city. If we are to believe the testimony of contemporary travellers, the Indian fascination with Europe was above all to create a showcase. Birdwood, who founded the Victoria and Albert Museum in Bombay, noted: 'Wealthy natives furnished their homes in the European style, but only the reception rooms, while they themselves lived apart, often in a separate building linked to the larger residence by a gallery or a covered bridge. Usually Europeans, like all other foreigners, were seen only in the public rooms, and only close friends were received in the private apartments.'

Some items of furniture were adopted by the Indians, such as the carved wood armchair with arm-rests and an extending foot-rest. This English invention known as the 'sahib's armchair' was to become the prerogative of India's rural nobility, who were prohibited from using upright chairs because of their similarity to thrones.

Maharajas and nawabs, imitated by industrial magnates and merchants, assuaged their passion for Europe in the many shops established in the major cities - Bombay or Calcutta - or in Europe's capital cities. Within India some firms founded by Europeans employed local craftsmen, famed for their skill. Thus the firm of Hamilton & Co., founded in 1808 in Calcutta by the British businessman Roger Hamilton, employed a large number of Indian gold and silversmiths, lapidaries and cabinet-makers. Using western models as the source of their inspiration, these craftsmen created Indo-European objects in the firm's workshops. Other famous stores such as Lazarus, J. Robert & Cie in Bombay, and The Emporium of Taylor in Calcutta kept well-to-do Indians and European residents supplied with furniture, silverware, glassware and *objets d'art*.

The Indian princes who rubbed shoulders with European high society on the race courses of Britain and in the casinos on the French Riviera belonged to the everyday mythology of the tabloid newspapers published on either side of the

English Channel. As wealthy as they were sybaritic, they boarded P. & O. steamers heading for Europe. Loyal and well-known patrons of the Ritz and other palatial hotels in London and Paris, they were accompanied by an impressive retinue of aides-de-camp, private secretaries, porters, several wives with their ladies' maids, their children and their nannies. Such journeys were less frequent before World War I because the princes were less westernized and the sea voyage was long, but between the two wars it was not unusual for visits to last three or four months each year. The princes ransacked the showcases at Asprey and Mappin & Webb in London and bought whole floors of furniture from Maples, the furniture firm founded in London in 1841, or from its Paris branch established in 1896.

In her book *A Princess Remembers*, Gayatri Devi, the daughter of the Maharaja of Cooch Behar and wife of the Maharaja of Jaipur, recalls the palaces of her childhood, residences in Calcutta and Darjeeling, jam-packed with objects brought back from all over the world: upholstered armchairs, chairs and tables from England and France, fabrics and ceiling lights from Italy, carpets from Kashmir, pink quartz and jade from the Chinese district in Calcutta. In fact it was an eclectic assortment of neo-classical and modern pieces which the princes brought back from their travels in Europe and which still leave an imprint on their palaces: huge rooms decorated with Corinthian columns, Victorian ceiling lights, French-style ceilings. . .

Watercolour by Christofle, 1878, for a bed ordered by the Maharaja of Bahawalpur. The Maharaja had insisted that there should be four different types of women at each of the corners of the bed: Parisian, Spanish, Italian and Greek. Christofle archives, Paris

Visits to Europe also provided the maharajas with an opportunity to place special orders with major firms in Paris and London, sometimes of an extremely extravagant nature. One of the most outlandish was addressed to the firm of Christofle, and ran thus: 'A wooden bed garnished with applied silver work part gilded, monograms and coats of arms, decorated with four lifesize bronze figures painted in flesh colours and with natural hair and moving eyes and arms, carrying fans and horses' tails; the bed must contain a harmoniphon music box with eight tunes, six cheerful and two melancholy.' The client insisted that his anonymity should be respected and came incognito to the rue de Bondy factory to check that his specifications had been fulfilled exactly before the bed was dispatched to him. The secret was indeed well kept, for it has only recently become known that the client in question was none other than the Governor of the State of Bahawalpur, S.M.K., standing for Nawab Sadik Muhammad Khan IV.

Another amazing piece, now in the Victoria and Albert Museum, was commissioned by the Maharaja of Mysore - Tippoo Sultan (1782-1799). This is a carved and painted wooden automaton of a tiger devouring a British officer as he lies on the ground, illustrating both the Maharaja's passion for tigers and his hatred of the British. The tiger's body conceals a miniature organ, probably made in France, that imitates the roaring of the tiger and the cries of the victim. The British seized the tiger on capturing Seringapatam in 1799 - its owner Tippoo Sahib died during the battle - and it then became one of the favourite attractions at the museum of the East India Company in London.

Even though Rudyard Kipling wrote that 'maharajas and nawabs were created by Providence to provide the world with picturesque settings, stories about tigers and grand spectacles', such extravagant commissions were nonetheless exceptional in the output of European firms.

Most Indians have an extreme passion for crystal and glass, an almost religious symbol of purity and translucency. The enormous ceiling lights and chandeliers installed in every room in maharajahs' palaces attest to this. In the nineteenth century, aware that this huge continent was proving the largest market in the world thanks to the immense wealth of the princes, the ultra-rich dynasties of merchants as well as the affluence of European residents, European firms sent agents to India or turned to intermediaries and the huge stores that imported western goods. The archives of Baccarat, the famous French crystal manufacturing company founded in 1764, record negotiations regarding the setting up of an agency in Bombay to be run by a businessman established in India who would know the country and its many languages. He would be assisted by an employee from the company's warehouse with a knowledge of crystal, able to keep Baccarat informed of any initiative that would satisfy the tastes of the company's well-to-do Indian customers.

Moreover there is a comment to the effect that 'good employees establishing special agencies in the main centres would create far more lasting resources for the future than can be entrusted to go-betweens who are no more than travelling businessmen'. While there is a note dated 30 September 1886 indicating that 'the plans for an agency in India are on the point of fruition', it is impossible to confirm that the scheme was ever implemented, in spite of an ambiguous

 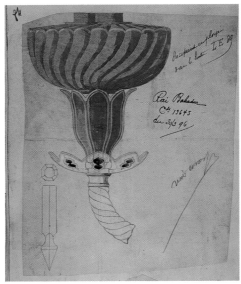

reference in 1888 to a Bombay agent. In fact special orders were transmitted through shops already established in India which sold as well as glass, porcelain, furniture and jewellery. The middlemen, who did not divulge their customers' names to Baccarat, or other European firms, unfortunately make it impossible for us to know who their eventual clients were. Thus in Baccarat's archives there is a record of an

Above: *watercolour of a decorated and cut crystal ceiling light designed by Baccarat in the early twentieth century.*
Right: *sketch of tulip-shaped glass chandelier casing made by Baccarat for Rai Bahadur in 1896.*

order for ten lamp globes placed in 1883 by Orr & Sons based in Madras. In July 1905 C. Flor & Cie of Bombay requested a price, without giving the client's identity, for ceiling lights in decorated and cut crystal, with 24 jets, 48 jets and 36 jets - the jets and globes frosted and oviform. On 10 August 1906 an English intermediary, Molineau Webb in Manchester, asked for an estimate for a crystal tomb, supplying a detailed drawing - only the parts marked in blue to be crystal, with the pedestal and tombstone in granite. An accompanying note states that 'this tomb is intended for an Indian raja who in all probability still has many years to live, which would allow us if the order is placed not to inconvenience you with regard to the delivery date'.

The ignorance of the present owners as to the precise origin of their possessions and the frequent absence of a signature make it difficult to attribute pieces correctly. Nonetheless there can be no doubt that many European firms exported glass and crystal goods to India - English, Belgian, French and Bohemian ceiling lights and chandeliers, Venetian mirrors, Murano glass - thanks to intermediaries established in India or purchases made in Europe by wealthy Indians or their agents.

In most Indian residences the huge rooms kept solely for storing porcelain services, some of them consisting of several hundred pieces, reveal a very strong liking for European tableware. A few specialist shops in Paris and London acted as go-betweens, the most highly regarded in Paris being Le Vase Étrusque, place de la Madeleine; Rouart which was later bought up by La Samaritaine; Bourgeois, rue Drouot; and Le Grand Dépôt which opened in 1863 in the rue Drouot, known as the 'palace of fired ware'; and in London John Smith's, Asprey and Maples.

The services, specially commissioned by the maharajas and frequently adorned with their coats of arms, were made after the choice of decoration had been agreed between the prince and the porcelain manufacturer, either through an agent or at meetings at society events in Paris or London. An anecdote regarding the special order placed by the Maharanee of Baroda with the Limoges porcelain manufacturer Charles Field Havilland in 1948, relates that when a hunt was held at the estate of the Countess of Montebello, the Maharanee supposedly gave Robert Havilland, then chairman of the company, a piece of her sari as a source of inspiration for the decoration of her service.

PHOTOGRAPHY

The first Indian photographic society was founded in Bombay in October 1854, soon to be followed by others in Calcutta and Madras. Thus, through the agency of its British administrators, only too happy to catalogue the riches of their colony, India adopted photography soon after it was invented, and from 1860 photographic firms started to take over from court painters. The number of companies specializing in landscape photography at the end of the century is revealing: twenty-four in Bombay, six in Madras and about ten in Calcutta. During the 1870s professional photographers set up studios respecting the constraints of purdah. A certain Madame Crick opened a studio exclusively for taking photographs of ladies in purdah in Calcutta, complying with the ban on any male presence. Then in 1862 Lala Din Dayal, a woman photographer attached to the Nizam of Hyderabad, announced in turn that she, too, was opening a studio reserved solely for women in purdah.

From 1860 most maharajas had British professional photographers attached to their courts, immortalizing their marriage ceremonies, their fleet of limousines or the delights of the zenana. Those most intrigued by the new discovery followed the example of Ram Singh II, Maharaja of Jaipur, taking lessons in the art of photography. Indeed, several portraits show us this reformer sitting in a *bergère* - instead of ensconced on the traditional throne, as was customary - wearing a turban and pince-nez, heavy gold anklets and patent-leather European-style shoes.

In some palaces which are now hotels these ostentatious photographs are often the only pictures hanging on the walls - alongside hunting trophies. Seen by the Indian princes as a court genre and a medium enhancing their standing, they reflect an implacable aura of majesty and continue to display the splendours of the princes' reign.

JEWELLERY

The worship of jewels was linked to the almost sacred or religious nature of precious and semi-precious stones and *pietre dure*, which were believed to have mystical properties giving them magic powers. For instance diamonds contain *maras,* powers that can increase sexual potency. Precious stones conferred power and health on their owners, who wore them in accordance with strict codes, or were not afraid to reduce their treasure by swallowing cocktails of pearls and crushed precious stones. Seemingly a Chinese traveller convinced the Maharaja of Mysore that one of the most effective aphrodisiacs was made from crushed diamonds, an assertion which risked seriously depleting his treasure.

Though occasional contacts were made between the maharajas and European jewellers in the nineteenth century - for instance with the English jeweller Hamilton in Calcutta, or a special order placed with the French jeweller Oscar Massin - it was not until 1910-20 that some princes were sufficiently impressed by European creations to decide to transform their legendary adornments worthy of *The Arabian Nights.*

The first sporadic contacts with Cartier were formed in 1911 in connection with the coronation of George V. Jacques Cartier embarked for India on the steamship *Polynesia* on a voyage lasting sixteen days via Malta, Port Said and Aden. The fob watches which were then all the rage in London and Paris also fascinated the Indian princes: the Nizam of Hyderabad chose a gold one, the Maharaja of Kapurthala a blue enamel one, the Maharaja of Nawanagar a platinum one, and the Aga Khan one set with diamonds. As for the Nawab of Rampur, he was attracted by a gold travelling clock with a striking mechanism that reproduced the sound of European cathedral bells, so attracted in fact that he bought four of the same model. Time-keeping instruments, watches, clocks and automata had been known in India since the eighteenth century thanks to the East India Company which offered them for sale at in its Lall Bazaar in Calcutta, along with other European goods.

At the beginning of the 1910s, the firm of Cartier was far-sighted enough to realize the potential development of import and export between India, Europe and America, entrusting business to the Bombay Trading Company and later, in the same spirit, to the European Watch & Clock Company.

While the wish of the Gaekwar of Baroda, Sayaji Rao III - who owned legendary diamonds such as the 'Star of the South' and 'Empress Eugénie' (given by Napoleon III to his wife, and previously the property of Potemkin, the favourite of Catherine the Great of Russia) - to have his whole collection of jewels reset in platinum by Cartier came to nothing, due to the resentment of Indian jewellers, one commission stands out as a major event in the annals of the firm. It relates to the Crown Jewels of the Maharaja of Patiala. During the 1920s, when Indian jewellery using enamel and cut or cabochon gemstones was becoming popular in Europe, the Indian princes for their part now dreamt only of having their fabulous treasures transformed in the Art Deco style to comply with European fashions. The beauty of Cartier's creations associating platinum with a wide range of materials struck the East with the same impact as the colours of the East had delighted Cartier. Indian princes' treasures took the form of precious stones and they wore fabulous jewellery of inestimable value; they were attracted by the novelty of platinum settings, platinum seeming to be a metal capable of setting off the depths and colours of the stones to even better advantage than gold. This was in spite of the symbolic value of gold,

Above: *studio study for a ceremonial necklace made in 1928 by Cartier for the Maharaja of Patiala. The centre of the necklace is adorned with the fabulous 234.69 carat De Beers diamond. Cartier archives, Paris.*

Left:: *necklace design in gouache on tracing-paper prepared by Cartier for the Maharaja of Nawanagar in 1931. Cartier archives, London.*

regarded as the celestial metal *par excellence*. From the 1920s on, Cartier's Bond Street shop in London, a favourite destination when the Indian princes went shopping, dealt with their orders. In about 1925 the Maharaja of Patiala entrusted his most valuable pieces to the parent company whose designers, while respecting the traditional Indian forms, were given the subtle and delicate task of

transforming them into an Art Deco style. Among the pieces were a large ceremonial necklace with the 234.69-carat Victoria or De Beers diamond as its centrepiece, nose rings made of precious stones typical of southern India, anklets, bracelets to be worn on the upper arm, and *hathphul*, wedding jewellery worn on the back of the hand linking a bracelet and rings, traditional to Rajasthan.

These fabulous Indian-cum-Art-Deco jewels, immortalized in a 36-page photograph album, were displayed at the rue

Above: *watercolour drawing of an emerald and diamond necklace made in 1928 by the Paris jeweller Boucheron for the Maharaja of Patiala. Boucheron archives.*

Right: *design for necklaces consisting of cabochon emeralds and platinum-mounted diamonds, made in 1928 by Boucheron for the Maharaja of Patiala. Boucheron archives.*

de la Paix in 1928 at an exhibition which was a major event the wealthy of Europe and America would not have missed attending on any account, and it was given wide press coverage.

To appreciate this Arabian Nights' treasure to the full, it should be added that over and above the work he had done by Cartier, the Maharaja of Patiala also approached Boucheron, entrusting the firm with six grey steel caskets enclosing a pile of gems simply wrapped in fine coloured cloths. Baron Fouquier who had arranged the meeting noticed the stunned reaction when 'white, yellow and blue-tinged diamonds appeared, then pearls and the most magnificent collection of emeralds imaginable (about 1800 carats). And finally sapphires and rubies.' A waterfall necklace, a mesh breastplate of diamonds set off by pear-shaped emeralds with a central 100-carat emerald surrounded by diamonds, a diamond crescent decorated with a ruby star - all these gems were given an Art-Deco setting that nonetheless respected the traditional oriental style.

There was another commission that rivalled the Maharaja of Patiala's, not in size but in the quality of the stones. It was placed by the Maharaja of Nawanagar, ruler of a small principality with its own pearl-fisheries on the Kathiawar peninsula, the least valuable pearls being crushed and used in traditional Hindu medicine.

The Maharaja commissioned Cartier to make a necklace of six rows of pearls, adorned with a 62.93-carat cut emerald, which could on occasion be transformed into a *sarpech,* or turban ornament. His remarkably fine collection of emeralds was reset into a fine ceremonial necklace composed of seventeen rectangular emeralds including one of 70-carats which had come from the coffers of the Sultan of Turkey; a necklace set with thirteen emeralds; two head-dresses, one adorned with a 25-carat emerald, the other with a 39-carat one; and a two-strand necklace of round emeralds.

Head-dress ordered from the Paris jeweller Cartier in 1926 by Maharaja Jagatjit Singh of Kapurthala. It consists of nineteen emeralds of various shapes, brilliants, rose-cut diamonds and pearls. The central hexagonal emerald weighs 177.4 carats, and the remaining eighteen a total of 254.84 carats. Cartier archives.

In 1926, a year before his golden jubilee, Jagatjit Singh of Kapurthala (1872-1949), so delighted with a head-dress he had commissioned from Cartier which had been created without any reference to European forms, commissioned a pagoda-style diadem. It is mentioned on 27 September 1926 in the entry in his diary, which he wrote in French: 'Lunch at the Ritz where I am introduced to the King of Yugoslavia, then pose in the studio of the painter Marcel Baschet in ceremonial dress, wearing a diadem.' He was so enthusiastic about watches and clocks that a palace employee had the full-time job of keeping them wound.

While some maharajas rushed to have their legendary collections of jewellery reset by the most highly regarded French or English jewellers in the first half of the twentieth century, some firms established in India had already turned to European models for inspiration in the nineteenth century. In Madras P. Orr & Sons employed local craftsmen who made jewellery of a composite Indo-European style, originally intended for Europeans living in India, and subsequently for native customers captivated by these rather hybrid creations. The use of claw settings for stones, a technique imported from Europe, was common, as was the technique of rose-cut diamonds or brilliants discovered by the Indian craftsmen, who merely polished the uncut diamonds.

LIMOUSINES AND LUXURY TRAINS

For centuries elephants had been the Indian princes' favourite means of travel. They had issued forth from the hand of the god Rama and were symbols of the cosmic order, embodying the pillars of the universe. Because of these divine attributes, the Maharaja of Mysore once a year prostrated himself in front of his oldest elephant, thus continuing the ancestral pact between his kingdom and the forces of nature which would in return shower prosperity on his subjects. Moreover, a sovereign's wealth and power were measured by the number of elephants he owned, sometimes as many as several hundred.

The car was to overturn this ancestral means of travel, relegating elephants

to ceremonial functions. The first car unloaded in India must certainly have been a French De Dion-Bouton ordered in 1892 by the Maharaja of Patiala - with the symbolic registration number 'O'. The Nizam of Hyderabad was fascinated by cars and built up a collection of some two hundred limousines: when he saw a car he liked on the road, he intimated to its owner that 'His exalted Highness would be immensely gratified to receive it as a gift'. Rolls Royce exported a variety of models to India: open tourers,

Above: *radiator cap in the form of a sculpted female figure made by Lalique for one the of the Maharaja of Wankaner's limousines.*

Right: *radiator cap from one of the Maharaja of Wankaner's Rolls Royces.*

saloon cars, coupés, estate cars and even vans - nearly eight hundred cars over a forty-year period. Most were custom-built, for some princes wanted to travel lying down, while washing, or even while holding cabinet meetings. The first Rolls Royce, known as the 'Pearl of the East', was bought by the Maharaja of Gwalior in 1908. The Maharaja of Bharatpur was intrigued, and in turn bought all the Rolls Royces on display in a showroom, engaging the services of an assistant whose job it was to drive the cars past him in succession - inside the palace. Maharaja Bhupinder Singh of Patiala owned up to twenty-seven Rolls Royces, in addition to one hundred or so other luxury limousines.

The Maharaja of Alwar owned a Lanchester, custom-built for him in Britain in 1924. Plated both inside and out, fitted with a carved ivory steering-wheel and driven by a chauffeur assisted by a mechanic seated on cushions made of gold thread, the rear bodywork was an exact replica of the

Radiator cap from another of the Maharaja of Wankaner's limousines.

coronation coach used by the British royal family. There is a story that the Maharaja of Alwar lent a solid silver model with aphrodisiac properties to a friend for his wedding ceremony. . .Another car was reserved for hunting wild animals, as Lord Mountbatten reports in his diary in 1921, after an escapade in the company of the Prince of Wales: 'The car went across wild country, going over potholes and ditches, weaving and rolling like a ship on the high seas, without ever having to move down into second gear.'

The emblem of the Hispano-Suiza - a stork in flight - prompted one Indian prince to buy ten of them, convinced that this symbol of fecundity would bring him happiness.

While most of the maharajas owned magnificent limousines, they were also fascinated by trains and had incredible railway coaches built for themselves, which were then coupled on to trains when they wanted to travel. The Maharaja of Indore, for example, ordered a coach in Germany to be decorated by the most renowned gold and silversmiths of the Paris firm of Puiforcat.

HUNTING AND SPORT

From the humblest to the richest, a strong sense of hospitality towards any stranger is something common to all orientals, and it was taken to extremes by the maharajas whose wealth meant they could indulge in any extravagance. In every Indian state, even the most unassuming, the guests' quarters were among the grandest buildings, fitted out with all the latest European conveniences. However, when such princely hospitality was extended to powerful members of the colonial hierarchy, ulterior motives could be at work: by honouring their European guests so lavishly, the princes put them in their debt.

Hunting, which by Indian tradition was the royal sport par excellence, turned out to be the most exciting attraction on offer to European guests and the maharajas made it a point of honour to organize outstanding events, especially beats in pursuit of the large cats, the source of so many far-fetched tales in western drawing-rooms, and so much tawdry writing.

From the second half of the nineteenth century the major European gunsmiths took advantage of the rivalry existing among wealthy hunters in so far as the splendour of their weapons was concerned. These became ever more magnificent, reaching a peak after World War II. The firm Holland & Holland was founded in London in 1835 and sent all its models to India to merchants such as Walter Locke & Co., Manton, Lyon & Lyon, and R.B. Rodda. Some models were ordered directly by the maharajas themselves who were extremely keen customers, among their number the maharajas of Jodhpur, Bikaner, Surguja, Barwani, Rewa, Mysore, Kapurthala, Patiala and Cooch Behar as well as the Nizam of Hyderabad. Holland & Holland supplied them with custom-made guns inlaid with ivory and precious metals, sometimes

Photograph of big-game hunters standing in front of their prey. Holland & Holland archives, Paris.

decorated with enamel. The gun-cases were just as splendid, made of crocodile skin with gold or silver mounts. As well as being magnificent the guns were extremely efficient: the Maharaja of Cooch Behar claimed to have brought down a bison with a single shot at a distance of eighty yards, while the Maharaja of Gwalior claimed to have killed 1,400 tigers in his lifetime, outdone by the Maharaja of Surguja who had accounted for 1,600. According to an Indian tradition every one of the hunting trophies piled up in the palaces was a witness to the hunter's victory over the evil spirits entrapped in the bodies of these fierce animals. While hunting with lances or spears was something that now interested only the intrepid, some shoots were regarded as unforgettable events and every hunter dreamt of being invited to such an occasion. One of the most famous was the annual ritual at Gajner, a property belonging to the Maharaja of Bikaner, when in the autumn, after an exhausting migration from the Arctic, thousands of sand grouse landed on the artificial lake, the only stretch of water in this arid region. According to Michael Sugich, when the Prince of Wales visited Gajner in 1905 the bag for one morning was over 100,000 birds.

In 1974, when the Nizam of Hyderabad's collection of 2,000 weapons was sold, Holland & Holland were given permission to examine them before buying several of the custom-made models. Three of the rifles, including one inlaid with gold, are on display at their London shop, while three others, including one decorated with an escutcheon set with the Nizam's coat of arms and monogram, are exhibited at their Paris shop.

Apart from hunting, sport is one of the pastimes most highly valued in Indian society. Except for polo, which was Asian in origin and had been played in the Punjab since the days of Alexander the Great, various sports are one of the remaining legacies of the British presence. Initially youngsters were initiated into golf, cricket, tennis, squash or hockey played on grass at school. A fair number of palaces had private tennis or squash courts, while some maharajas had their own polo or cricket teams.

Simla
Chapslee

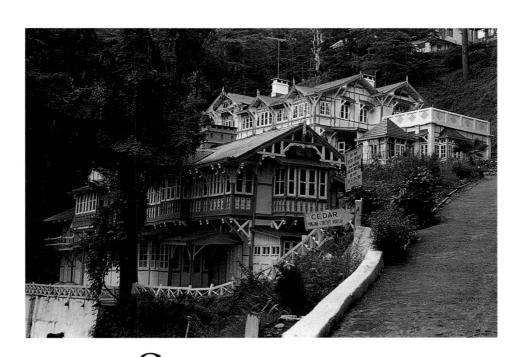

*S*imla, the capital of the state of
Himachal Pradesh, lies 2205 metres above
sea level on the slopes of the Himalayas. It still
bears the signs of the time when it was highly
regarded as a holiday resort by the British
and the Indian upper classes.

S IMLA WAS 'DISCOVERED' by Lieutenant Ross in 1819 and soon came to be highly regarded as a holiday resort by the British. Even though it is 1800 kilometres from Calcutta, from 1865 the town was the seat of government of British India during the sultry summer months. Lying 2205m metres above sea level and built on a crescent-shaped crest - some districts cling to precipitous slopes, virtually hanging in a void - Simla became the scene of a lively social life: the viceroy and his administration took up residence, there were endless balls and dinners, people played golf, tennis and polo. Writing his recollections of his journey to India in the 1870s in *L'Inde des rajahs* Rousselet relates: 'Calcutta is relegated to the status of a mere provincial town, and from the end of March until the beginning of October the only name that figures at the top of the Official Gazette and on viceregal decrees is that of Simla.'

It was in 1836 that Dr. Blake, an employee of the East India Company, sold the Governor-General Lord Auckland and his nephew Captain W.G. Osborne, a secretary at the War Office, two of the many properties he had acquired in Simla. After Lord Auckland's two sisters had transformed one of the chalets into a very comfortable residence, the hill where it stood was given the name Elysium Hill. The other chalet, Secretary's Lodge, renamed Chapslee in 1858 by its new owner, Colonel Peter Innes, was bought by Raja Charanjit Singh of Kapurthala in 1939. Chapslee was then totally refurbished: the walls were renovated using traditional Himalayan techniques (quarry-cut stones, mud and wood) and electricity and plumbing were installed. The Edwardian-style interior decoration was embellished by furniture from the family's other residences or designed by local craftsmen.

After Charanjit Singh's death in 1970, his grandson Kumar Ratanjit took over the property and his wife Promoti opened a girls' school to make running the property a profitable proposition, and soon Chapslee became a residence for paying guests.

Drawing-room decorated in the European style, with an upright piano and a tapestry.

Portrait of Maharaja Kanwar Suchet Singh of Kapurthala.

Entrance hall, with Edwardian-style furniture.

Crystal carafes and glasses with a palmette decoration in the Charles X style, made c.1830 by Baccarat.
Opposite: *dining-room, the table set in the European manner.*

Patiala
Sheesh Mahal Palace

*L*ying *about 100 kilometres from Chandigarh,*
Patiala has a group of magnificent palaces,
reminding us of its past as the capital of
a Sikh principality.

T HE TOWN OF PATIALA was founded in 1764 by the Sikh warrior Raja Baba Ala Singh; it lies on a hill called Prasthala, the hill evoked in the famous epic *The Mahabharata*, located in the former 'Brahmwarta' area discovered by the Indo-Aryans who found all the riches of nature there - fertile land, plentiful water and a mild climate. As a highly visible symbol of this Sikh state, the immense fort of Androon Qila was merely a starting point for the construction of many palaces financed by the successive heirs of the dynasty.

The name of Narinder Singh (1845-1862) is still linked with the building of the Moti Bagh Palace, or 'Pearl of Palaces', in the 1850s. This series of linked self-glorifying buildings, breathtakingly extravagant in scale, occupied a surface area of four hectares: four Durbar Halls, some three hundred bedrooms, fifteen dining-rooms. Banquets were held regularly, prepared by 150 cooks, including seventeen chefs whose sole responsibility it was to prepare the famous Punjabi curry. The palace, which is really more like a village in size, illustrates the taste for excess of its successive owners. Bhupinder Singh (1900-1938) collected wives as well as dogs, limousines, the most magnificent jewels and medals and decorations from every country. His many wives, freely conceded to him because of droit de seigneur - the fact that nobody knew exactly how many wives fed the legend - enjoyed huge private apartments for themselves and their children who were counted by the dozen. In addition there were lodgings for the legion of male and female servants employed to wait on them. The dogs, too, were treated with every consideration: they were kept by the hundred in a special pavilion equipped with the most up-to-date sanitation. If the recollections of the writer Maud Diver are to be believed, the palace in its vastness 'made Versailles look like a cottage: the huge state drawing-room was furnished with English chairs and day-beds, and decorated mainly with photographs of the crowned heads of Europe enhanced by the most costly frames . . . bedrooms the size of reception halls, and bathrooms the size of ballrooms.' The Maharaja's delusions of grandeur knew no bounds: sports, entertainments and celebrations punctuated his daily life and the lives of his distinguished guests. As a keen cricketer, he kept a personal cricket team at his court; as an ardent music-lover, he could call on an orchestra attached to the palace; as a collector of animals, he had a zoo containing the rarest species installed in the park.

Bhupinder Singh passed on this taste for magnificence to his son, Yadavinder Singh (1938-1974). However, rather than sharing his father's frenzied passion for women, he indulged in the less expensive joys of athletics; he was a university champion on several occasions, and was elected President of the Olympic Committee after Independence. However, this major political turning point in the subcontinent eventually sounded the death knell for the fabulous destiny of the maharajas, and the extravagance of their life styles inevitably forced some of them to sell their palaces to the state. This was to be the fate of Moti Bagh Palace, which was transformed into a sports' centre in accordance with the wishes of Yadavinder Singh. Then in 1959 he built another more modest palace known as the New Moti Bagh, to which the most valuable furniture and *objets d'art*, as well as other items regarded as specially sacred because of their associations with Sikh history, were transferred.

ERECTED BY
BURN & Co ld
HOWRAH

Suspension bridge built by Burn & Co. in 1887.
Opposite. *Sheesh Mahal Palace, a fountain-candelabra made by the British firm Osler.*

Sheesh Mahal Palace. Above: *European-style decanters. The two outside examples were probably made by Baccarat c.1860.*
Below: *details of the crystal sofa shown opposite.*

Above: *crystal sofa in a small drawing-room in the Sheesh Mahal Palace.*
Overleaf: *the Qila Mubarak, a former fort in Patiala, has been turned into a museum, with a collection of weapons, chandeliers and portraits.*

Kapurthala
Villa Buona Vista
Jagatjit Palace

*T*his diminutive fortified Himalayan
town, located in the Punjab about 100 kilometres
from Amritsar, boasts a huge palace
inspired by Versailles.

KAPURTHALA, IN THE NORTH-WEST of India on the Punjab plains, and the capital of the former Sikh state, became the fief of the Ahluwalia family after a quantity of land had been reconquered by Raja Jassa Singh. At the time of the Indian Mutiny in 1857 the British authorities rewarded Randhir Singh for his military support by strengthening his power. His death in 1870, followed seven years later by the death of his son Raja Kharak Singh, brought a five-year-old child to the throne: Jagatjit Singh. While British commissioners acted as regents, the boy was given a western-style education in France and England. Unlike most Indian princes who were Anglophiles, Jagatjit Singh developed such a keen passion for France and French culture that he bought a home in the Bois de Boulogne. His love for the French language was so great that he learnt to speak French fluently and throughout his life kept his diary in French.

These Francophile feelings reached their height when Jagatjit Singh decided, after visiting Versailles, to have a replica palace built on the plains of the Punjab - a building he named the Palais de l'Élysée, designed by the French architect A. Marcel. From 1902 for seven years, a large number of European and Indian craftsmen worked on the site. Each of the hundred or so apartments reserved for guests bore the name of a French town or celebrity. The interior decoration, embellished with porcelain based on Sèvres models, copies of Gobelins tapestries and Louis XV furniture, and Aubusson carpets ordered specially to fit the rooms, indicates the extent of Jagatjit Singh's admiration for French eighteenth-century art. The walls of the Durbar Hall were decorated with carved woodwork combining oriental and French motifs, and the carved ceiling, decorated with a stained-glass panel, was illuminated by small star-shaped lights; halfway up the wall, with balusters at regular intervals, was a gallery reserved for the ladies of the court when official ceremonies were held. The park, inspired by Le Nôtre's gardens at Versailles, was maintained by about five hundred gardeners.

The eccentricities of this Indian 'Sun King' did not stop at the confines of his property, for he built small villas in the surrounding area which looked as if they had been uprooted from the French countryside and transplanted in the Himalayan plains. French was declared the official court language, and the Prince's children on occasion wore powdered wigs, lace ruffles, silk breeches and pumps with buckles.

After Independence, Jagatjit Singh's successors were unfortunately obliged to sell this Versailles-style folly to the Indian state and it was converted into a military college - except for a few rooms that wistfully recall a splendour now gone for ever. Some of the furniture and *objets d'art* were transferred to the Villa Buona Vista a few kilometres away on the banks of the river Beas. This house was built in 1894 by J.O.S. Elmore, a British government engineer, and was used as a hunting lodge before being occupied by the Spanish Ranee, one of Jagatjit Singh's four wives. Today his grandson, the present owner of the villa, is the enthusiastic guardian of the furniture and *objets d'art*.

Above and below: *the front and back façades of Villa Buona Vista, the current residence of Maharaja Jagatjit Singh's grandson.*
The villa now houses many objets d'art *and items of furniture that came from the Jagatjit Palace.*

Opposite: *the dining-room at Villa Buona Vista with a portrait of Maharaja Jagatjit Singh by a French painter.*

*Villa Buona Vista: one of a pair of early twentieth-century French porcelain vases,
this one decorated with a portrait of the Maharanee of Kapurthala.*

Villa Buona Vista: paired porcelain vase decorated with a portrait of the Maharaja of Kapurthala.

Jagatjit Palace. Above: *English-style dining-room.* Below: *neo-rococo state apartment, probably inspired by the oval drawing-room at the Hôtel de Soubise, with copies of Louis XV furniture, and a French musical wall clock giving the date, the position of the planets and the time in many of the world's cities.* Opposite: *the Durbar Hall with the ladies' gallery.*

Villa Buona Vista. Above: *coloured photograph on glass of Maharaja Jagatjit Singh's four children.*
Below: *tripod table decorated with a portrait of Madame Récamier surrounded by portraits of twelve contemporary beauties.*

Villa Buona Vista: enamelled and gilded glasses, the paintings on porcelain transferred to the glasses.
Possibly from northern Bohemia, c.1900.

Villa Buona Vista. Above: *Venetian vase made in the 1870s by Salviati and a portrait of Maharaja Jagatjit Singh.* Below left: *photograph portrait of one of the Maharaja's wives, a Spaniard.* Below right: *portrait of the Maharaja's fourth wife who was Hungarian.*

Opposite: *in Villa Buona Vista a French gilt-wood console table in Louis XIV style, inspired by a model by Lepautre, with a photograph of Nehru on top.*

Rampur
Hamid Manzil Palace
Present day residence

*T*his former fief of the Rohilla dynasty,
east of Delhi in Uttar Pradesh, owes its fame
to the Hamid Manzil Palace which houses
one of Asia's greatest libraries.

THE WALLED TOWN OF RAMPUR was founded in 1623 by Shah Alam and Hussain Khan who came from Afghanistan and fought against Mogul supremacy. However, the state of Rampur, controlled by the Rohilla dynasty, was for a long time subordinate to Oudh, a richer and larger state. It was only in the second half of the nineteenth century, when Oudh had ceased to exist as a state and Murshidabad lost influence after the administration of affairs was transferred to Calcutta, that the Nawabs of Rampur emerged from the shadows and embarked on ambitious architectural projects. Thus in 1877-8 Nawab Muhammad Kabl-i Khan rebuilt the Jami mosque, and his successor, Nawab Hamid Ali Khan (1896-1930), engaged the services of the British engineer W.C. Wright - commemorated by a statue in the town - to produce plans for several palaces, a Durbar Hall and public buildings, designed in an Indo-European style similar to the palaces of Lucknow. The Durbar Hall, which has become one of Asia's greatest libraries, includes a huge gallery decorated with marble sculptures of nude female figures. It is reached by a long corridor the walls of which are lined with recesses each holding a sculpted female figure. Except for the public library, the complex of buildings is deteriorating as the years go by. The Nawab of Rampur's descendants now live in a colonial-style bungalow on the edge of the town.

Hamid Manzil Palace.
Opposite: *entrance corridor leading to the Durbar Hall.*
Overleaf left: *a chandelier in the Durbar Hall*

Today's home of the Nawabs of Rampur's heirs. Above: cut-glass lamp of European origin dating from the early twentieth century.
Below: bottles from a toilet set on either side of a jug made in Turkey or Bohemia for the eastern market.
Previous page right: Portrait of the Nawab of Rampur beside a vase made by the Belgian Val-Saint-Lambert company in the 1920s.

Today's home of the Nawab of Rampur's heirs. Portrait of the Nawab flanked by a pair of Venetian vases, with a crystal deer below.

Lucknow
La Martinière

*L*ucknow, now the capital of Uttar Pradesh,
played an important historical role in the eighteenth
century when the Nawabs of Oudh held sway; great
patrons of the arts and literature, they were
influenced by European scholars.

L IKE OTHER OF HIS CONTEMPORARIES from humble families who went overseas to seek their fortune, Claude Martin from Lyons disembarked at Pondicherry in 1751. Taken prisoner in 1761, he then enrolled in the East India Company's army before entering the service of Asaf ud Daula, Nawab of Oudh, for some time. Martin was a soldier-adventurer who also had a sharp business sense, and he subsequently amassed such a large fortune in the space of a few years that he was able to give financial support to the Nawab himself - after enriching himself at the Nawab's expense. He was also extremely powerful in his influence on the Nawab.

Following the example of the Indian princes whose wealth and power were measured by the splendour of their palaces, Major-General Claude Martin had an impressive château - originally intended to be his mausoleum - built to his own design in Lucknow. Although it was not completed until after his death in 1800, Martin nonetheless decided to live in part of it while it was being built. 'Constantia', the name of the palace carved on a first-floor balcony, was part of Martin's personal motto: 'Labore et Constantia' (Work and Steadfastness). Today the chateau-like building is known as La Martinière.

With numerous statues of Roman goddesses, gargoyles and Corinthian columns, the building freely combines Gothic and Italianate influences with Indo-Moslem elements. In the reception rooms the crystal chandeliers imported from England are reflected in the huge mirrors lining the walls. Paintings by Johann Zoffany - a German artist and friend of Claude Martin, French carpets and marble tables from Italy were scattered through the palace. Plaster friezes depicting figures from Greek mythology are such good imitations of Wedgwood ware that for a long time they were thought to have been imported from England. Scrutiny of Claude Martin's letters, in which a large number of orders for plaster of Paris are recorded, has recently revealed that in fact Indian craftsmen drew inspiration from Wedgwood models to perfect these friezes.

In his will the extremely wealthy adventurer specified not only that the château should be turned into a school, but that two other schools should be founded - in Lyons and Calcutta - to commemorate his name.

Tower facing the château La Martinière.

Dining-room decorated with plaster friezes imitating Wedgwood ware.

Above and below: *drawing-room ceilings decorated with plaster Wedgwood-like friezes.*

Dining-room with a painting depicting the palace and a portrait of one of the school's headmasters.
Opposite: *main hall of the Husainabad Imambara, a Moslem building constructed in Lucknow by Muhammad Ali Shah in 1837.*

Calcutta
Marble Palace
Mullick Palace
Yule Bank
Mitter Palace

Now the capital of West Bengal, Calcutta
is known as the 'city of palaces' because of the
dozens of splendid western-style residences built by wealthy
Indians. The town itself is a three-century-old British
creation, and was the capital of British
India until 1911.

T HE MARBLE PALACE is one of the few of the 150 or so patrician dwellings which nineteenth-century Bengali society could boast had not fallen into a state of disrepair. Now, attacked by dust and pollution, strangled by chaotic urban growth, the peeling façades of other such palaces indicate that they will soon disappear altogether. The survival of the Marble Palace is due to its founder, Raja Rajendro Mullick Bahadur (1819-1887), who decided to bequeath his property to the gods. Since then the family has shared the revenues from their heritage with no risk of either the real estate or movable property being sold off.

It was Jayram Mullick, an ancestor of Raja Rajendro Mullick, who originally settled at Govindapur. The town was 'discovered' by Captain John Charnock who, in 1690, decided to establish a trading post there on behalf of the East India Company; it was also frequented by the Portuguese, Dutch, Danish and French. This favoured site, made up of three villages, was the genesis of the future Calcutta; lying on an arm of the Ganges delta, it provided safe anchorage for sea-going ships. In 1757, after Fort William was built, a plot of land in the north district was conceded to the Mullick family by the government authority, and named Pathuriaghata.

The Mullick family made their fortune four generations later, Gangavishnu Mallick having embarked on trading in silver, gold and sugar. Unlike other prosperous merchant families, the Mullicks were motivated by a strong feeling of philanthropy: Gangavishnu in particular founded charitable clinics and rest centres which proved invaluable during the terrible famine of 1770.

The education of Gangavishnu's grandson Raja Rajendro Mullick (who was nearly three years old when his father died in 1821) was entrusted to an English tutor, James Weir Hogg, who introduced Rajendro to European art. Though they did not lead him to neglect the philanthropic aspirations he had inherited from his predecessors, Raja Rajendro developed two passions: art and natural history. When he was sixteen he started building a neo-classical palace conceived as a 'Temple dedicated to Art and Beauty'. It illustrates the aesthetic canons then fashionable in Calcutta, particularly the juxtaposition of composite ornamental elements derived from the European baroque and neo-classical styles.

Raja Rajendro was so involved in the building of his palace that he took personal charge of the five hundred native and foreign craftsmen working on the site for five years. A huge area of the park was set aside to create a zoological compound housing rare animals and birds - Calcutta's first zoo.

This huge residence, named the Marble Palace by Lord Minto in the early twentieth century, is typified by a chaotic accumulation of *objets d'art*: large Ming vases, copies of Sèvres vases, Venetian goblets, alabaster candelabras and Roman and Greek sculptures reflected endlessly in huge mirrors, along with copies of Rubens, Van Dyck or Veronese hanging side by side, offer visitors the aesthetic manifesto of a collector fascinated by Europe.

While part of the palace is still reserved for the family's private use, a large number of state apartments are open to visitors. If they come shortly before noon they will see the daily meal served to some five hundred of the city's poor. The philanthropic mission continues.

Above: *a palace in the north of Calcutta in the residential area occupied by wealthy Indians in the nineteenth century.*
Opposite: *Marble Palace courtyard. The cast-iron garden furniture was supplied by the British Army & Navy Stores.*

Marble Palace. Above: *detail of the inside courtyard. On the left a statue of Diana the Huntress.*
Opposite: *gallery overlooking the courtyard.*

Marble Palace. Above: *drawing-room with nineteenth-century sculptures. The glass cases are copies of eighteenth-century European cases.*
Opposite: *the same neo-rococo drawing-room with a carved gilt-wood Venetian mirror. In the centre case, a vase inspired by Meissen porcelain.*
Overleaf left: *copies of European paintings hung in the imposing drawing-room.*

Marble Palace. Above: *portrait of Queen Alexandra, with a neo-eighteenth-century sculpture of a woman wearing a tricorn in the foreground.*
Previous page right: *the billiard room showing an Art Nouveau lamp and two Chinese Imari-style vases.*

View in the Marble Palace garden which houses western and oriental statuary.

Mullick Palace: gallery decorated with a series of identical statues of the 'Crouching Venus'.

Mullick Palace. Above: *detail of the gallery showing copies of antiquities made at the end of the nineteenth century.*
Below left: *copies of eighteenth-century sculptures at the entrance to the palace.* Below right: *a copy of 'The Three Graces' by Canova in the entrance.*

Mullick Palace. Above left: *first-floor drawing-room. The sculpture is a copy of one of Marie-Antoinette.*
Above right: *first-floor drawing-room with a copy of the 'Winged Mercury'.*
Below: *in the first-floor drawing room a porcelain and bronze vase, made in the late nineteenth century after French models.*

Mullick Palace: first-floor drawing-room.
Overleaf left: *façade of a Mullick family palace in north Calcutta.*

Yule Bank, a residence near Calcutta. Above: *drawing-room furnished with a clock and other items made of cut crystal,
probably by the English firm Osler.* Previous page right: *the garden bordering Calcutta's Hoogly river.*
Opposite: *detail of a late nineteenth-century clock decorated with a painting depicting Eros and Psyche.*

Mitter Palace: porcelain vases made in the late nineteenth century after French models.

Mitter Palace: drawing-room decorated with a Venetian mirror.
Overleaf: *view in the garden of Kathgolee House, the residence of a Jain merchant at Murshidabad.*

Above: *neo-classical façade of Kathgolee House.*
Opposite: *façade of a palace in north Calcutta*

Delhi
Rashtrapati Bhavan
Princess of Bikaner's
residence

Delhi, the capital of India since 1911,
has two contrasting faces: the lively bazaars of
Old Delhi, the original town, and the wide straight
avenues lined with bungalows in the residential
and administrative districts.

ALTHOUGH DELHI has not always been the capital of India it has nonetheless played a crucial role in Indian history. The Hindu epic *The Mahabharata*, written 3000 years ago, mentions the existence of Indraprastha, a town located more or less on the site now occupied by New Delhi. But Delhi is not a city belonging to the Hindu tradition; it developed following Moslem invasions, with both Turks and the Afghans having left the mark of their wealth and power on its architecture.

Delhi has twice been the capital of an empire: under the Moguls from the seventeenth century, then under British rule after 1911. Reversing the decision of earlier Mogul emperors, who in the sixteenth century chose Agra, Emperor Shah Jahan transferred his capital to Delhi in 1638. He then built two of the most spectacular of the city's buildings: the Red Fort and the Jama Masjid, or 'Friday mosque'. Under British rule, Delhi was eclipsed by Calcutta, the capital of the Bengal region that had become a British colony in 1773, and the British government's decision to transfer the Indian capital to Delhi was not made until 1911, during the famous visit to India by George V.

Seen as an imperial capital by the English architects Sir Edwin Lutyens and Herbert Baker, Delhi is built in red sandstone and white marble in an eclectic style combining European and Mogul ornamental conventions. Work was interrupted during World War I, so New Delhi was not officially inaugurated until 1931. The Rajpath, an extravagantly wide and long avenue embellished with pools of water, leads to the Rashtrapati Bhavan, the vice-regal palace which became the residence of President of the Republic of India after Independence. Built on rising ground, Raisina Hill, the palace is preceded by the two Secretariat buildings, one on either side of the Rajpath, and now the headquarters of the main central government ministries. The fact that two architects were involved, in spite of their differences regarding the height of the buildings, has had no marked effect on the unity and harmony of the whole: Herbert Baker designed the Secretariat buildings and the Parliament, and Sir Edwin Lutyens the Rashtrapati Bhavan. The excessive size of the latter - it has 340 rooms - meant that servants were compelled to travel through the basement of the palace on bicycles.

The British government assigned seven plots of land at the eastern end of the Rajpath to the most notable princes, but the authorities insisted that designs for residences there should be submitted for approval so as to ensure the stylistic unity of the area as a whole, which was given the name Princes' Square. The two most splendid palaces, those of Hyderabad and Baroda, are the work of Sir Edwin Lutyens, who drew up plans for three further palaces; other buildings were entrusted to followers of Lutyens. The stylistic unity of these princely palaces, reminiscent of that of the Rashtrapati Bhavan, is derived from the combination of classical, European and indigenous decorative elements. Hyderabad Palace is on two floors, with a butterfly-shaped plan, a recurrent feature in the English architecture of the time, which is repeated at Baroda Palace.

These palaces became the property of the Indian state after Independence, and today are official government buildings.

Overleaf left: *Rashtrapati Bhavan sculpture of an elephant at one of the entrances to the south wing of the palace, near the Jaipur column.*

Princess of Bikaner's palace. Above: *two large cut-crystal and gilt-bronze bowls made by Baccarat in 1878 for the Universal Exhibition. In the background, an Empire-style clock depicting the 'Chariot of the Sun'.*
Below: *pair of crystal vases in Venetian style made by Baccarat in 1841, and reissued by the firm a century later.*

Opposite: *Princess of Bikaner's palace, detail of one of the cut-crystal and gilt-bronze Baccarat bowls.*
Previous page right: *baldaquin-style bed of cut-crystal bought in Calcutta and now in a Delhi palace*

Princess of Bikaner's palace. Late nineteenth-century lamp with a sand-blasted glass shade
depicting an English landscape; English porcelain coffee and tea service.
Opposite: *detail of a painting by G.G. Rötig, 1920s.*

Colonial-style bungalow built in the 1920s in the residential district of New Delhi. Above: *bedroom*.
Below: *library/sitting-room furnished in the English style*.

Opposite: *drawing-room furnished with silver furniture and a large crystal mirror*.

Colonial-style bungalow: entrance furnished with a silver armchair and a Venetian mirror made of cut and engraved crystal.
Opposite: *monogrammed crystal scent bottles*

Pataudi

*T*his peaceful little town lying south
of Delhi, away from the tourist routes, is the
proud possessor of a palace built in the mid-nineteenth
century and a neo-classical-style residence built in the
1930s by an Austrian architect.

Before independence, Pataudi was one of the many small states scattered across the country. The maharajas, rajas or nawabs of all those states, large or small, who had accepted a British presence before Independence were allowed to keep their thrones provided they recognized Britain as the supreme power. In return, they relinquished control of external affairs and defence and were guaranteed internal autonomy.

The Nawab of Pataudi, who ruffled old traditions by marrying the Princess of Bhopal for love, had a new residence built in the 1930s, giving the commission to the Austrian architect Heinz who designed a neo-classical building.

The huge rooms are arranged round two internal courtyards with a fountain in the centre of each. The architect solved the problem of keeping the rooms cool by designing wide, marble-paved verandas facing one another and supported on a series of columns which overcome the oppressive heat by allowing air to circulate.

One of Heinz's neo-classical style verandas in the Pataudi residence.

Above: *portrait of the Princess of Bhopal, wife of the Nawab of Pataudi.*
Below: *table with European place settings, porcelain dinner service decorated with the family coat of arms, cut-crystal glasses and silver-gilt cutlery.*

Opposite: *entrance hall furnished with a stuffed tiger and a pair of silver armchairs.*

Above: *bathroom with fittings imported from England.*
Opposite: *bedroom.* Overleaf: *hand-painted straw blinds on the veranda.*

Dholpur

*T*his small capital city of a former
principality, located not far from Gwalior
in Madhya Pradesh, has a residence that is striking
because of its architectural originality: red-brick
façades are combined with very ornate,
eastern-style ironwork.

U NDER BRITISH RULE there were in fact two Indias: the India made up of the provinces, administered from the capital (Calcutta, then New Delhi), and the India of the 565 princely states.

Some princes, such as the Nizam of Hyderabad and the Maharaja of Kashmir, ruled over areas as large and populated as the major European countries, while others governed states barely larger than a village. The combined surface area of more than four hundred of the princely states was no more than 30 square kilometres.

Dholpur is the former capital of the principality of the same name which was founded in 1805. Compared with many enormous palaces - a prince's power being gauged by how many palaces he had and how many rooms in each - the Maharaja of Dholpur's residence seems quite modest, even though it was enlarged in the second half of the nineteenth century. The building's originality lies in the materials used: the long, austere façades of red brick provide a striking contrast with the very ornate ironwork of the balconies.

During the 1920s the walls of the entrance hall and most of the first-floor rooms - small sitting-rooms, bedrooms and bathrooms - were covered with painted tiles imported from Europe, probably from England. Friezes of fruit trees, birds in flight and farm animals form the decoration of some rooms, while others are decorated with stylized motifs in different colours in the form of scrolls or waves.

View into the English neo-Adam style main drawing-room.

Rooms lined with tiles, in patterns inspired by the designs of William Morris, probably imported from England in the 1920s.

Tile details in the first-floor vestibule.

Tiled bathroom with fittings imported from England.
Opposite: *bedroom. Each room in the palace is tiled in different tones.*

Gwalior
Jai Vilas

*T*he history of the city of Gwalior,
in Madhya Pradesh, is part of the Rajput saga.
Following the decline of the Mogul empire in the
mid-eighteenth century it became a fief of
the Scindias, a Maratha dynasty.

DURING 1858 AND 1859, in the aftermath of the Indian Mutiny against the British, there were a large number of bloody uprisings in India. In Gwalior the Ranee of Jhansi, stripped of her states by the East India Company, led the local rebellion. She met her death on 17 June 1858 beneath the fortress walls, her weapons in her hands, while exhorting the troops to launch a final assault. The rebellion of this Indian Joan of Arc was the opportunity for the Scindia Maharaja of Gwalior to demonstrate his personal loyalty to the British, in spite of the fact that his own troops had mutinied. Once he was sure of keeping his throne, he started rebuilding the town at the foot of the former fortifications, and had a new palace built - Jai Vilas, 'Palace of Victory'.

The Maharaja, Jayaji Rao Scindia, entrusted Colonel Michael Filose - better known in India as Mukel Sahib - with building the palace, and the Colonel set off for Europe to study royal architecture in the European capitals and acquire the materials, furniture and decorative objects - with no financial limits on his budget. Thus chandeliers, tapestries, mirrors, paintings, furniture and fabrics were imported from Europe.

A few figures suffice to give some idea of the huge scale of the palace, which covers a surface area of 305,000 square metres. The Durbar Hall, reached by a two-flight staircase and a balustrade made of twisted crystal, is 30 metres long, 15 metres wide and the height to ceiling 12.5 metres. Because of the room's enormous size, the carpet was woven on site by convicts. Two crystal chandeliers imported from Europe, each 13 metres high, each weighing 3 tonnes and having 248 holders, are reflected in the huge mirrors hanging along the walls - a third chandelier is in store to allow for breakages. Installing these two chandeliers was so tricky that elephants were first weighed, then taken up on to the roof terrace one by one, to be sure that the ceiling could support the weight of the chandeliers.

The most extreme flight of fancy relates to the state banqueting-room. At receptions, on a table which can seat two hundred people, an electric-powered solid silver miniature train ran round on a 100-metre-long rail carrying whisky, port, liqueurs and cigarettes. If one of the crystal bottles was taken off the train would stop, although the Maharaja could speed up the train or prevent it from stopping if he so wished. There is a famous story about this strange attraction: during a banquet given in honour of the viceroy in the 1930s a short circuit caused the train to run off the rails, showering whisky and liqueur all over the table and the guests in their evening dresses and dinner jackets.

While Jayaji Rao Scindia enjoyed extravagance, he felt rather lost in the two hundred-room Jas Vilas palace, so he built a more modestly proportioned residence, the Moti Mahal, where he preferred to stay.

Above: *internal courtyard with a fountain made by the English firm Osler.*
Opposite: *entrance hall.*

Silver train made by the English company Armstrong Whitworth & Co., carrying cut-crystal bottles.
The chairs are decorated with the family crest, a sun flanked by two cobras.

Neo-classical style banqueting-room with the train and track on the dining table.

Above: *first-floor landing above the entrance hall. The twisted crystal balustrade was probably made in Belgium.
In the background, a portrait of a member of the Scindia family.* Opposite: *state drawing-room showing the
248-light chandeliers purchased at the end of the nineteenth century at a Universal Exhibition.*

Detail of the state drawing-room decorated with a huge cut-crystal candelabra and furniture in the Napoleon III style.

Details of the state drawing-room. Above: *portrait of a member of the Scindia family.*
Below: *ivory photograph frames in the shape of the family crest.*

*The entrance hall. Above: a crystal chandelier with one hundred lights, probably
made in Belgium at the end of the nineteenth century.
Below: detail of the frieze running below the crystal balustrade, the palmette decoration in a
neo-classical style with crystal stars, pendants and brilliants*

Opposite: *late nineteenth-century cut-crystal cheval glass, sofa and chair.*

Jaipur
City Palace
Dunlod

*J*aipur, the capital of Rajasthan, known
as the 'pink city', is surrounded by huge walls
inside which the roads intersect at right angles. Many
palaces, built from the eighteenth century onwards,
bear witness to its glorious past.

ONCE HIS MIND had been set at ease by the decline of Mogul power, Sawai Jai Singh II decided to leave his hillside fortress near Amber and move his capital into the plain. He founded Jaipur on 18 November 1727, a date precisely determined by the court astrologer, and entrusted the design and planning of the town to a Bengali priest who was initiated into the mysteries of sacred architecture. Drawn along the lines of a *mandala* or religious diagram, with a grid of straight avenues demarcating the districts, each reserved for a particular activity, Jaipur is encircled by a crenellated wall. Apart from the pink sandstone buildings, the town was painted pink (a colour symbolizing hospitality) in 1875 to celebrate a visit by the Prince of Wales, later Edward VII.

The palace at the heart of Jaipur consists of a large number of buildings separated by courtyards, including the Mubarak Mahal, a pavilion added at the end of the nineteenth century by the British architect Samuel Swinton Jacob. A marble door flanked by elephants leads into the Diwan-i-Khas, or audience chamber, inside which two large solid silver jars made in 1896 are on display. Each weighing 345 kilos and holding 9000 litres, they were used to carry the Ganges water required for Sawai Madho Singh II's ablutions when he travelled to England in 1902. The court of the Diwan-i-Khas leads to the Chandra Mahal, or Moon Palace, the seven floors of which include the private apartments of the present owner, furnished in the European style.

The Rambagh, a palace lying outside the town, was famous as the setting for receptions by which the cream of early twentieth-century European society set great store. Originally this property was only a modest garden belonging to Sawai Ram Singh II's governess. He became heir to the State of Jaipur - on his father's death in 1835 - when he was only one year old, and the British regency council built a pavilion here with the idea of occasionally getting him away from the clutches of the zenana. When he became the owner on his governess's death in 1856, he used the pavilion as a country house and shooting lodge. Sawai Madho Singh who succeeded him in 1880 was involved in schemes for enlarging the building throughout his reign. Thus during the first decade of the twentieth century, about ten suites, a banqueting room, a reading room and a reception room were added to the twenty or so original rooms. The architectural design was again entrusted to Jacob, who served as Chief Engineer for the State of Jaipur from 1867 to 1902 when he became the Maharaja's personal adviser. The ornamental elements - arcades, *jaali* or openwork stone screens, *chattris* or open kiosks - contribute to the palace's elegance, highlighted by the milky whiteness of the marble.

After Sawai Madho Singh's death in 1922 the Rambagh was used as a school for his son, Sawai Man Singh II, who later made it his official residence. A start was made on its modernization and the construction of extra buildings intended to house the zenana. As the Maharaja was a great sportsman and an international polo champion, he equipped the palace with unique sports facilities: a polo ground, an indoor swimming-pool, and tennis and squash courts. The palace employed in the region of four hundred servants, some solely assigned to hunting the pigeons which caused damage to the buildings. It is now a hotel.

Internal courtyard of the City Palace.
Opposite: *City Palace: Chandra Mahal Baranda, a gallery decorated with painted walls and portraits of Maharajas of Jaipur.*

State drawing-room, City Palace. Above: a bowl and birds by Lalique.
Below: a gilt-bronze table centrepiece in the neo-classical style, probably made in the mid-nineteenth century.
Opposite: under-lit rectangular table by Lalique between two similar square tables.

State drawing-room, City Palace. Above an exotic silver candelabra and a portrait of the present Maharaja.
Opposite: *solid silver furniture.*

L YING BETWEEN JAIPUR AND BIKANER, Dunlod is an old fortified town deep in the Thar desert. Moslem tribes occupied the Shikhavati area somewhere around the fourteenth century, and the towns that developed there became important trading centres. Encouraged by the English, the Marwari merchants gradually extended their business activities throughout India. We have them to thank for the amazing decorations that embellish the façades and interiors of their family homes. While these include scenes from Indian mythology, there are also images the inspiration for which the Marwaris found on their travels throughout British India and in cities like Bombay and Calcutta where they had to live for business reasons: portraits of British rulers, trains, cars, bicycles, and western technical innovations like the gramophone and the telephone.

The palace at Dunlod was built in 1750 by a descendant of Sheka of Amarsar, the young king who gave his name to the Shikhavati region. The exterior architecture is purest Mogul, the *duchetta,* the semi-circular balcony housing the apartments of the women kept in purdah and the boxes from which they could view spectacles, was furnished in the Indian style, while the eclectic decoration of the state drawing-room combines Louis XV and Chippendale styles. The private apartments, located on either side of the central wing of the palace, were decorated in 1930s European style.

Upper gallery overlooking the main drawing-room.

Durbar Hall detail with a portrait of Sawai Madho Singh II, father of the present Maharaja of Jaipur.
Below: *a corridor (left) and games room (right).*

Opposite: *drawing-room with Louis XV style gilt-wood furniture*

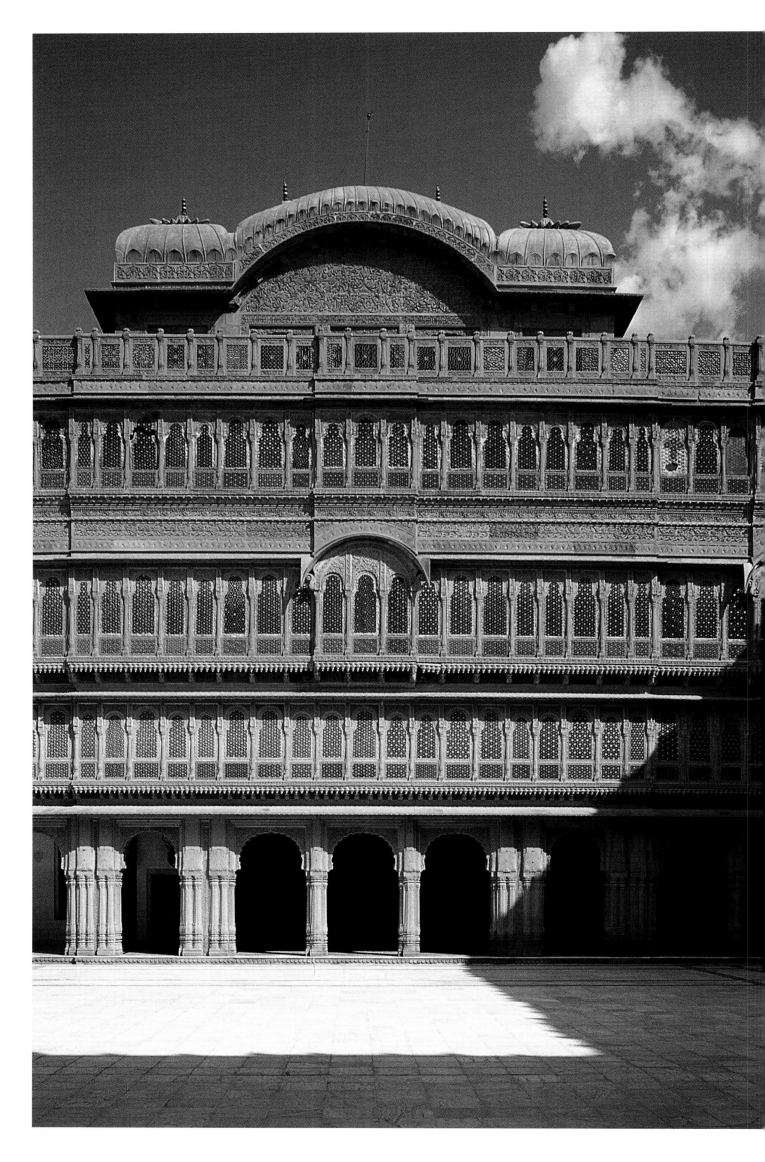

Bikaner
Lallgarh Palace

*B*ikaner, located in the north of
Rajasthan, was once an important staging
post on the caravan route. The former fortress and the
Indo-European palace are built in the same pink-red
sandstone as the buildings in Jaipur.

BIKANER WAS FOUNDED IN 1465 by Rao Bika, the second son of the ruling family of Jodhpur. As the younger son, who would never succeed to the throne, he carved out a fief of his own in the Thar desert area - chosen because of the opportunities offered by the passage of caravans. The conquest of his territory was underpinned by the building of an impressive fortress in 1485. Over the years, the descendants of the Rathors, a Rajput clan, managed to hold the kingdom together, and as a result many pavilions, financed by the maharajas who succeeded one another to the throne, were annexed to the fortress.

Four centuries later, a descendant, Ganga Singh (1887-1942), was one of the exemplary Indian princes who were given English-style educations. Combining Victorian virtues with proud Rajput chivalry, he embodied extreme good taste with a fierce fighting spirit, and a great passion for things modern with an unswerving attachment to the traditions of his heritage. As Ganga Singh succeeded to the throne when he was only seven, a regency council directed by a British agent took control of any government decisions during the prince's minority, and he was educated at the famous Mayo College at Ajmer. It was not for entirely disinterested reasons that the British government established a number of exclusive schools reserved for the local aristocracy in India; modelled on English public schools, these institutions instilled loyalty towards the British Empire and 'modern' ideas of the West into the Indian princes. And since the British regarded the influence of the women enclosed in the zenana on young princes as pernicious, the regency council decided on Ganga Singh's behalf that a new palace should be built at a distance they considered sufficiently removed from the zenana.

The scheme was entrusted in 1896 to a British officer in the Indian Army and Chief Engineer of the State of Jaipur, Samuel Swinton Jacob, who had made a name for himself publishing a reference book on Indian architecture, *Jeypore Portfolio*, in 1890. Jacob set about drawing up plans for the palace, assisted in the scheme by the Chief Engineer of the State of Bikaner.

Built in pink sandstone, the palace was named Lallgarh Palace by Ganga Singh in honour of his father, Lall Singh. In its design Jacob combined ornamental elements typical of the Rajput style with Mogul architectural references. The façades alternate openwork stone screens with slim columns and embrasures with a purely decorative function; the huge terraced roofs are topped with numerous small octagonal pavilions. The internal space is divided into three distinct areas, a traditional feature of Rajput fortresses: the Durbar Hall - or public reception hall, the Maharaja's private apartments, and the zenana, each having its own entrance. The part of the palace reserved for important visitors drew its inspiration from colonial European homes: as well as the bedrooms and western-style bathrooms, this area includes a series of rooms devoted to traditional European pastimes - a billiard room, a smoking room, a games' room and a music room.

The decoration of the palace is a tribute to nineteenth-century European eclecticism. There is absolutely no connection between the architecture of the palace and the Belgian mirrors, the Bohemian chandeliers, the Louis XV and Victorian-style furniture, the Greek and Roman sculptures, the jade *objets* and the oriental vases. All these European furnishings make an unlikely match with the Mogul style wall decorations in the palace.

Lallgarh Palace was turned into a hotel in 1972, but a part is still kept as private accommodation for the family. In one of the drawing-rooms a magnificent European *objet d'art*, acquired in 1930 by Ganga Singh, is on display: a crystal boat made by Baccarat for the 1900 Universal Exhibition. A symbol of the entry of Paris into the twentieth century, the boat is embellished by two cherubs, one at the prow astride a chimera gazes towards the horizon, the other at the stern loosens a mooring rope.

Gajner Palace: located in the desert beside an artificial lake, this is one of the few resting places for
migratory birds, so the palace was a favourite with the great European and Indian shots.
Lallgarh Palace. Opposite: *detail of the crystal and bronze boat made by Baccarat. In the background a painting depicting the Lallgarh Palace.*

*Only two examples of the crystal boat were made by Baccarat for the exclusive Paris shop Le Grand Dépôt. Made to coincide
with the 1900 Universal Exhibition, the vessels were designed by the sculptor Charles Vital-Cornu and symbolize the entry of Paris into
the twentieth century. Dismantled down to its component parts, this example was transported to Bikaner, in 1930.
Lallgarh Palace.* Opposite: *detail of the crystal Baccarat vessel showing the gilt-bronze cherub casting off the mooring rope.*

Lallgarh Palace: hunting photographs exhibited in the palace museum.

Lallgarh Palace: drawing-room decorated with hunting trophies.

Jodhpur
Umaid Bhawan
Sardar Samand

*L*ying on the edge of the Thar desert,
after Jaipur, Jodhpur is the second largest city in
Rajasthan. The former fortress and the huge palace in
Indian Art Deco style built in the 1930s dominate
the old town and its teeming life.

IN 1547 RAO JODHAJI, a descendant of the Rathors, a Rajput clan which had ruled over Mandor since the thirteenth century, decided to found a new capital bearing his name: Jodhpur.

The Rathors were regarded as virtually invincible warriors: of all the conquerors who swept over northern India they were the only ones not to be stopped - not even by the Mogul Emperor Akbar, who was forced to enter into a treaty with them. It is thanks to Prince Pratap Singh (1845-1922) that the name of Jodhpur achieved worldwide renown. As founder of the Jodhpur Lancers, he fought for fifty years at the side of the British in Afghanistan, China and Egypt, and during World War I he and his Lancers annihilated enemy German positions near Cambrai, France.

Umaid Singh (1903-1947), faced with an unprecedented drought in 1920, embarked on a campaign of major public works in his state, building canals and roads, sinking wells, building temples and palaces, so that his subjects would be paid a wage. It was then that he decided to build a palace that would outdo all other architectural follies in its magnificence and dimensions. After consulting the most distinguished architectural authorities over this ambitious scheme, he approached the partnership of Lanchester & Lodge in Great Britain. Henry Lanchester, a disciple of Edwin Lutyens, had made his name in designing a large number of public buildings, in particular Cardiff and Deptford town halls, hospitals in London and Birmingham and the Methodist Central Hall in Westminster, London.

Court astrologers, who were consulted as to a propitious site, chose Chittar Hill on the side of the plain across from the former fortress. The first stone was laid by the Maharaja on 18 November 1929 and building work continued for about fifteen years, continually employing 3,000 local workmen and craftsmen. Huge blocks of sandstone were extracted from a quarry about twelve kilometres away, and brought to the site by rail. Masons cut the five-ton slabs in such a way, numbering them as they went, so the stones could be assembled without using any mortar.

The originality of the palace, a textbook example of Indian Art Deco architecture, lies in the clever combination of pre-Islamic and Art Deco ornamental elements. The 195-metre-long façade is arranged in two symmetrical wings round a central axis topped by a double dome 56 metres high. The 347 rooms are distributed between several buildings assigned to different functions: reception rooms, guest apartments, the Maharaja's private apartments, the zenana, administrative and service offices, servants' quarters. There are eight dining-rooms, a banqueting hall accommodating three hundred people, numerous kitchens, including kitchens given over specifically to the preparation of English, French and Chinese dishes, a games room, a library, a recreation room, and a heated, scented swimming-pool. The royal suites are decorated with frescoes by the Polish artist Julius Stefan Norblin who stayed in the palace for several months.

As all the furniture and air-conditioning equipment, ordered in Britain just before the outbreak of World War II, was bombed in warehouses or torpedoed at sea by German military forces, local craftsmen made all the furniture, drawing their ideas and inspiration from European models; they also perfected a traditional air-conditioning system of openwork stone screens with cold water travelling through the stone.

Umaid Singh moved into his palace at the end of the war, but died shortly after in 1947. The death in 1952 of his eldest son in an aeroplane accident brought his other son Gaj Singh to the throne at the age of four. Gaj Singh inherited a grandiose palace which in time seemed to him to be completely excessive, and it was lived in very little until 1977 when it was converted into a luxury hotel, the Maharaja keeping one wing for his private use.

Above: *Art Deco style bathroom in different coloured marbles.*
Opposite: *bedroom decorated with a fresco by the Polish artist Julius Stefan Norblin.*

Frescoes in an Indo-European style by Julius Stefan Norblin.

Above: *bedroom, the screen painted by Julius Stefan Norblin. In the background a console table by Raymond Subes.*
Opposite: *crystal fountain, from the Saint-Louis crystal works, in the first-floor hall.*
Overleaf left: *Art Deco lamp-stand and portrait of Gayatri Devi, Maharanee of Jaipur*

Above: *Art Deco light furnishings and fittings in a bedroom* (left) *and dining-room* (right).
Below: *paintings by Norblin in one of the palace drawing-rooms.*

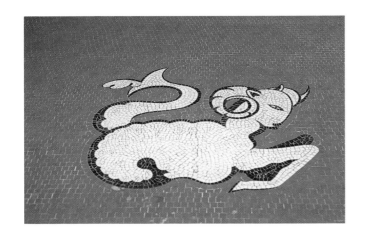

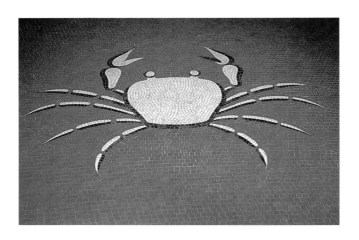

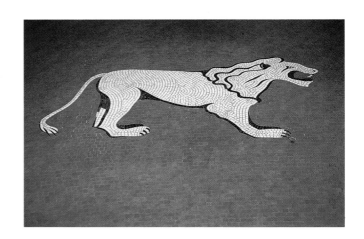

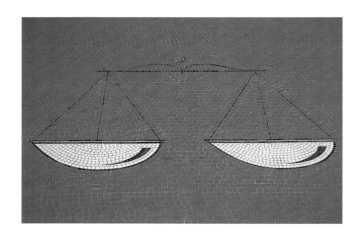

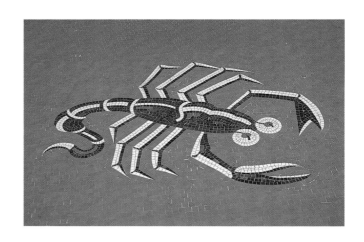

Above: *mosaic signs of the Zodiac decorating the swimming-pool.*
Opposite: *the swimming-pool located in the palace basement.*

Sardar Samand: a hunting lodge belonging to the Maharaja of Jodhpur near Umaid Bhawan Palace.
Above: *bar decorated with a fresco by Norblin and steel furniture upholstered with panther-print fabric.*
Opposite: *lamp-shade made up of hunting photographs.*

Baroda
Lakshmi Vilas

Until Independence Baroda, in east Gujarat,
was the capital of the principality of the Gaekwar of
Baroda. These feudal rulers typified a paradox that was
common at the time: while they were traditionalists in their
extravagant taste for luxury, they were sufficiently modern-
minded to embark on large public
works programmes.

T HE GAEKWARS, OR 'PROTECTORS OF COWS', came to power in the eighteenth century, and the following century entered into a treaty with the British guaranteeing them complete authority over their territory. This dynasty was one of the inner circle of five principalities most honoured by British protocol, the importance of their rulers being acknowledged by a 21-gun salute at official ceremonies.

The Lakshmi Vilas palace - the name comes from the goddess of wealth and beauty - was built in the state of Baroda by Gaekwar Sayaji Rao III. Building of the 160 metre long palace was started in 1878 to designs by the English architect Charles Mant, and was not completed until 1890. During this time, the architect Robert Fellowes Chisholm had been called in to replace Charles Mant who had committed suicide, afraid that he had got his calculations wrong and that the building might collapse. Mant had arrived in India in 1859 with the Royal Engineers, and had designed the palaces of Kolhapur and Darbhanga; he is regarded as the inventor of the Indo-Saracenic style, of which Lakshmi Vilas is a perfect example.

Stylistic eclecticism is everywhere in the palace interior, for in mixing traditional Indian and European decorative elements, the decoration of the palace required the services of a large number of western craftsmen. Twelve Venetians spent eighteen months at Baroda laying the floor mosaics in the Durbar Hall, which is lit by stained-glass windows made to order in England. The marble used for the floor of the vestibule and staircase was imported from Carrara, the gildings and mouldings on the walls and ceilings were carried out by craftsmen from London, the garden was designed by an English landscape designer, and the sculptures in the vestibule and the Durbar Hall are by the Italian sculptor, Felici.

Entrance hall in an Indo-Italian style, the floor composed of several different marbles.
Overleaf: the Durbar Hall with a Neo-Islamic style ceiling and stained-glass windows made to order in England.

Above: *chest of drawers' top in* pietre dure.
Below: *floor mosaic, crafted by Venetians in the Durbar Hall, depicting the coat of arms of the dynasty.*

Opposite: *first-floor gallery.*

Shell depicting Hercules and the serpents, carved in cameo style.

Display cabinet with figures inspired by Meissen porcelain.

Above: *one of the first-floor drawing-rooms.*
Below: *another first-floor drawing-room with neo-Louis XVI style furniture and a large painting in the style of the French painter Hubert Robert.*

Opposite: *on the wall a neo-rococo decorative trophy in gilded wood.*
Overleaf: *terrace opening on to the park.*

Wankaner
Ranjit Vilas Palace
Oasis House

Lying in the state of Gujarat about
50 kilometres from Rajkot, the old town of Wankaner
is dominated by a group of palaces built on the hill. The
most recent of these, constructed at the beginning of
the twentieth century, is a odd mixture of Gothic,
Graeco-Roman and Indian styles.

THE RAJPUT CLAN OF JHALA has ruled over Wankaner for nearly four hundred years, but in the second half of the nineteenth century, Raj Sahib Bane Sinh (1860-1881) decided to leave the town and his ancestral palace and take up residence on a hill overlooking the plain. From then on it was there that the successive homes of the dynasty would be built. Bane Sinh's son, Raj Sahib Amar Sinh (1887-1947), who was still a child when his father died, was looked after by a regency council and brought up in the English tradition at the school for princes in Rajkot, his western education being rounded off by a grand European tour in 1899.

Although he built a new palace, Amar Vilas, from 1900 to 1907, he regarded it merely as a stop-gap home leaving him full leisure to design another palace which he regarded as his life's work. Giving instructions to the Chief Engineer of Wankaner, he freely mixed the most unusual architectural elements - Doric, Ionic, Gothic, Indo-Saracenic and Palladian - and his unbridled imagination gave rise to one of the most extravagant palaces. Ranjit Vilas Palace is a three-storey building topped by a tall clock tower, crowned by a marble dome and flanked by open kiosks with columns and hypostyle rooms. The Maharaja combined red sandstone from the Wankaner quarries with various marbles extracted in India or imported from Carrara and Belgium. The first stone was laid in 1907, but the first celebration to be held there did not take place until 1928 on the marriage of the Maharaja's son and heir Raj Sahib Pratap Sinh, born the same year as the first stone was laid. Work had been slowed down by World War I, and the prohibitively high cost prompted the Maharaja, who did not want to place a heavy burden on his country's finances, to carry out the interior furnishing by stages; the firm commissioned to do this work was John Roberts & Co of Bombay.

Independence sounded the death-knell for the sumptuous life style which the Maharaja and his family had been used to. In the early 1970s, because of the inescapable presence of tourism in Gujarat, Raj Sahib Pratap Sinh and his son and heir, Dr. Digvijay Sinh, decided to receive paying guests in their palace.

Ranjit Vilas Palace. Opposite: *detail of the drawing-room.*

Ranjit Vilas Palace. Above left and below: *detail and view of the dining-room decorated with hunting trophies.*
Above right: *silver armchair standing in one of the drawing-rooms.*

Ranjit Vilas Palace: library/drawing-room with English furniture.

Ranjit Vilas Palace: entrance hall. The hunting trophy is made from the tusks of the elephant shown in the photograph.

Ranjit Vilas Palace. Above: *detail of a drawing-room with English-style furniture.* Below: *billiard room.*

Ranjit Vilas Palace. Above: *bathroom with fittings imported from England.*
Opposite: *two-flight staircase in the Indo-Italian style. The staircase is so designed that a person on one flight cannot see anyone on another.*

I F WE STOP FOR A MINUTE to consider the vast scale of most of these palaces, it is easy to understand that maharajas liked to get away from them from time to time. Lying near a river a few kilometres from his main residence and surrounded by a luxuriant garden, the pavilion built by Raj Sahib Bane Sinh no doubt answered this desire for solitude.

His son Raj Sahib Amar Sinh also enjoyed staying there, and used it to house his distinguished guests. In 1917, when his daughter married Purna Chandra Bhanja Deo, a Maharaja from Orissa, the pavilion was given the name Purna Chandra Bhawan and later came to be known as Oasis House.

In the early 1930s, Raj Sahib Amar Sinh instructed the Chief Engineer of Wankaner to enlarge the pavilion, adding reception rooms, bedrooms and suites, following a U-shaped ground-plan surrounding an enclosed garden. From the mural paintings to the furniture, and the *objets d'art* to the tableware, the interior decoration of the Oasis House is an oriental reinterpretation of the rules of European Art Deco.

Although the family still go there, the pavilion is also used by paying guests. During the summer months visitors to Oasis House can keep cool inside the *baoli,* or stepped well: occupying three underground levels and kept cool by a huge pool fed by a fountain, small rest rooms and covered galleries make it possible to escape there from the intense, sultry heat.

Oasis House: dining-room, looking through an open door to a drawing-room. Friezes made by local craftsmen follow late Art Deco patterns.

Oasis House. Above: *one of the many bedrooms, embellished with painted wooden furniture inspired by European Art Deco.*
Below: *view of the dining-room.*

Opposite: *detail of the bedroom. Each of the rooms in the Oasis House is decorated with a different frieze.*
Overleaf: *first-floor bathroom made by the Scottish firm Shanks.*

Oasis House. Above: *indoor swimming-pool in a wing of the pavilion.*
Opposite and overleaf: *the* baoli, *or stepped well, constructed in the park of Oasis House.*
The pool keeps the underground galleries and rest rooms cool during the months of sultry heat.

Morvi

*M*orvi in western Gujarat boasts
a huge fort built in the old town at the end
of the nineteenth century. It is linked to an
Art Deco palace on the other side of the
river by a long suspension bridge.

A T THE BEGINNING of the twentieth century Waghji Ravaji (1879-1922), nicknamed the Black Pearl Prince, was one of the first rulers to travel to Europe, thus transgressing the taboo associated with crossing the oceans (referred to as 'the Black Water' by Indians), and so risking exclusion from his caste and being considered impure in the eyes of orthodox Hindus. This daring traveller, enamoured with the new western technological discoveries, undertook a huge modernization programme in his capital and built an enormous palace in the Indo-Moslem style, thus confirming the good reputation of builders from the Rajput clans. His son Lakhdhirji (1922-1948) was responsible for one of the most amazing Art Deco palaces; along with the palaces of Indore and Jodhpur, it is regarded as the most outstanding example of this style to be built on the Indian subcontinent.

After traversing hundreds of miles of arid desert landscape and passing only a few herds of goats and caravans of camels, the traveller cannot help but be struck by the incongruity of this palace, rising like a mirage induced by exhaustion from the interminable journey. The palace was designed by the Indian architect Ram Singh; building work started in 1931, and finished about ten years later. Resembling a liner at anchor or embedded in sand, and inspired by the architecture of Le Corbusier and Mallet-Stevens, the palace is built in the form of a huge square inside which there are two open courtyards surrounded on all sides by columns, with a circular fountain playing coloured water at the centre of each. The severity of the external façades is relieved by rotundas at the four corners of the building. The central entrance portico, supported by marble columns and topped by a tower, leads into a wide vestibule the ceiling of which is decorated with a circular coffered fresco depicting the 'Chariot of the Sun' painted by Julius Stefan Norblin (whose name is also linked with the palace at Jodhpur). The ground floor is divided into several guest apartments and reception rooms - drawing-rooms and dining-rooms. One of the dining-rooms, unusual for its extremely elongated rectangular shape, has a large number of French windows opening on to both of the courts. There are two bars, survivals from the cocktail era, one on the ground floor decorated in an unusual pink and contrasting with the chrome furniture, the other on the roof terrace between the two courts, decorated with a marble fountain and furnished with small benches facing one another, a reminder of the furnishing arrangements in trains and luxury liners of the period. The billiard room and games room, which open on to one of the courts, are next to an enormous indoor swimming-pool - the water supplied from a marble fountain - decorated with panels of sand-blasted glass and engraved with aquatic motifs, behind which there is a gym. The first floor is reserved solely for the private apartments which are arranged round a huge dining-room.

Archive drawings indicate that the furniture was specially ordered for each room. While the architecture of the Art Deco palace at Indore can still be seen, all the furniture (made by the great names of the period: Ruhlmann, Eileen Gray, Le Corbusier, Da Silva Bruhrs) was sold at a Sotheby's sale in Monte Carlo in 1980. The interior decoration of the palace of Morvi, on the other hand, is still in place, the furnishings were supplied by the top firms in London and Paris, or made in Bombay to English designs.

Above: *detail in the entrance hall of the ceiling fresco painted by Julius Stefan Norblin, depicting the 'Chariot of the Sun'.*
Below: *two of the four stuffed wild animals in the entrance hall.*

Opposite: *gallery opening on to one of the two courtyards.*

Sand-blasted glass panel dividing the swimming-pool from the gym, decorated with a mermaid riding a large fish.

Detail of the marble swimming-pool.

Above and opposite: *two of the four wall frescoes by Norblin in the swimming-pool.*

These two paintings, with two other frescoes facing them at the opposite end of the building, flank a fountain supplying water to the swimming-pool.

Above: *billiard room, with a painting by Norblin*. Below and opposite: *overall view and detail of the games room, the furniture of painted wood, steel and leather. On the wall, a painting by Norblin.*

Overleaf: *ground floor bar, with a wall painting by Norblin.*

Above and below: *two of the palace's many bedrooms, the one below with a large fresco by Norblin.*
Opposite: *the main staircase with its illuminated staircase.*

Above: *one of the dining-rooms, with a painting by Norblin and a lacquered wood and metal table.*
Below: *study/library with wood panelling and a painting by Norblin.*

Opposite: *leather and painted wood chairs bearing the family coat of arms. On the table, a crystal candlestick by Baccarat.*

Above: *one of the ground-floor drawing-rooms, furnished with armchairs in sea-green lacquered wood.*
Below: *fresco by Norblin decorating the upstairs bar.*
Opposite: *smaller fresco to the left of the bar depicting a flamenco dancer.*

Above and below: *first-floor bedroom decorated in shades of blue.*
The furniture is embellished with circular Art Deco motifs.

Opposite: *dressing-table in the bedroom, the mirror, decorated with white and blue-tinted circular motifs, reflecting two tester beds.*

Ootacamund
Southwick

*T*his hill station, 2286 metres above
sea level in Tamil Nadu, was much appreciated
during the hot weather by the British, who left behind
numerous reminders of their presence.

OTACAMUND, A FAMOUS HILL STATION in the west of Tamil Nadu and commonly known as 'Ooty', was discovered by the British in the first half of the nineteenth century when they took up residence in the nearby village of Kotagiri. Perched at a height of 2286 metres on the green slopes of the Nilgiri Hills, Ooty is surrounded by mountains covered with thick forests towards Mysore, and with tea and coffee plantations in the direction of Coimbatore.

The town became one of the favourite resorts of the British during the hot summer months. Renowned for its coolness and pleasant way of life, it also became the summer residence of the Madras government, even though Madras was about 500 kilometres away. In this remote region occupied by the Toda, Kota and Kurumba tribes, the British could not wait to reproduce authentic stone cottages, lay out carefully tended gardens, golf courses and cricket grounds, and build private clubs and select schools. And it was in this lush Eden transformed into an English town that the rich Saith Moslems, who were driven out of the semi-desert regions of Gujarat in 1882, chose to settle, buying up half the land in the space of a few years.

Southwick, a symbol of their dazzling success, is a huge residence built at the end of the nineteenth century on the Wellington Road. As a tribute to the three founding fathers of the dynasty (Andul, Rahim and Sait), their initials and the name of the estate are outlined in stags' antlers on a wall in the billiard room. Their most precious mementoes, especially those commemorating a pilgrimage to Mecca, are displayed in the wedding room, the floor of which is paved with pottery shards depicting secret signs, using a technique perfected by Andul and carried on by sons and grandsons.

Inside the drawing-room, a huge room plunged in semi-darkness, Chinese furniture made of black cherrywood, a Chinese carved cedarwood screen, a black marble Italian table and a Swiss clock reveal that, like the Indian princes, the owners took pleasure in combining European and oriental furniture. There is a curious tradition that again emphasizes their eclecticism: all the men in the dynasty are depicted in photograph portraits with one hand resting on a Japanese chair above which is a mirror that belonged to Marie-Antoinette. The European influence is still more pronounced in the private apartments - games room, sitting-room, bedrooms and bathrooms - which are decorated in 1930s style.

Wedding room, the floor paved with pieces of broken pottery using a technique perfected by the family.

Detail of the floor of the wedding room.

Drawing-room decorated with Chinese furniture.

Above and opposite: *the billiard room. On the wall antlers outline the name of the
property and the initials of the three men who founded the dynasty.*

Mysore
Amba Vilas

*T*he city of Mysore, perched 770 metres
above sea level, was until Independence the fief
of the Maharajas of Mysore, a principality that
covered a third of modern Karnataka.

M YSORE, THE FORMER CAPITAL of the state of Mysore, was the fief of the Wodeyar dynasty until 1759 when Hydar Ali, a military officer belonging to the family, usurped the throne. Tippoo Sultan succeeded his father in 1782, but was killed in 1799 during a battle with the British who were laying siege to the nearby fortress town of Seringapatam. The British restored the Wodeyar dynasty in the person of a five-year-old child, Krishna, assisted by a tutor and a family council, and the construction of a fortress celebrated the re-establishment of legitimate power.

After a fire which devastated a major part of the building in 1897, it was decided that the English architect Henry Irwin should be asked to design a new palace. Completed in 1912 and enlarged in 1932, it is regarded as one of the most extravagant examples of the Indo-Saracenic style, typified by a large number of dome-topped turrets arranged around a central tower. An unusual feature is the metal framework and iron columns, made by the British company Macfarlane of Glasgow, used in building two state reception-rooms. While most of the five hundred rooms in the palace, the marble floors inlaid with jasper, cornelian and lapis lazuli, the carved Burma teak ceilings, the pillars topped with multi-lobed arches, and the solid-silver door panels, conjure up the Orient of *The Arabian Nights*, a few of them are based on European decorative models.

Detail of a frosted glass screen.

The Maharaja's study with English-style furniture. On the wall a collection of fly-whisks.

Dining-room furnished in the English-style.

Above: *details of decorative features in the palace.*
Below and opposite: *view and detail of one of the drawing-rooms, showing an organ and the portrait of a former Maharaja of Mysore.*

Hyderabad
Falaknuma Palace
Chauwmohalla Palace
Purani Haveli Palace

*F*ormerly the capital of one of the grandest of India's principalities, since Independence Hyderabad has been the capital of Andhra Pradesh. The old fortified city, still encircled by its walls, has a large number of palaces bearing witness to its mighty past.

AFTER IT WAS ESTABLISHED IN 1591, Hyderabad quickly became a great centre of Moslem power in the Deccan and was occupied by the Moguls from 1687. The state owes its autonomy to the governor Asaf Jah who broke away from the Mogul empire in 1724, adopting the title of Nizam ul Mulk. On his death in 1748 internal struggles broke out at the court of the princes of Hyderabad, with the French and British intervening to try to establish their 'claimants'. Dupleix was eventually disowned by Louis XV and recalled in 1754, while Robert Clive established his claimant on the throne.

It was the Prime Minister, Nawab Vikar ul Umra, who built the Falaknuma - 'Mirror of the Sky' - Palace at the end of the nineteenth century, on a site discovered during an annual feast held at Bibika Chasma, where sterile women went in search of fertility. As with many other cosmopolitan princes fascinated by the West, it was the Nawab's dream to engage a European architect. The palace was completed in 1883 after seven years, during which the Nawab lived in a pavilion on the south of the hill to supervise progress. It has been claimed that he built the palace to win the favours of a fickle woman, but he was to live there for only five years: the sixth Nizam, Mir Mahbub Ali Khan, urged him to hand over the palace - together with its furniture and *objets d'art*. A large debt, combined with the Nizam's jealousy, apparently lay behind this 'transaction'.

The general ground-plan of the palace, lying on Kohi-Tur Hill at the edge of the town, forms the shape of a scorpion. The superstitious came to believe that this motif (visible only from the air) was the explanation for the misfortunes that befell the architect and the palace's successive owners: the architect died accidentally aboard a ship bound for Italy; the originator of the palace was poisoned, while the sixth Nizam had a fatal rocking-chair accident. From the streets of the town the palace stands out against the sky like a mirage in stone, and as you draw nearer the full measure of its splendour is revealed.

Facing north because of the intense heat, the façade is Palladian in inspiration with a huge double-flight staircase leading to the ground floor. There, a veranda leads into a large marble entrance hall with a fountain. Beyond the hall is the library, modelled on the library at Windsor Castle, and on the same floor, beside the sixth Nizam's private office, is a state bedroom furnished in western style which was used by the Nizam himself, then kept for royal visitors - including the Duke of Windsor, when Prince of Wales, and the Archduke Ferdinand of Austria.

This arrangement of the rooms was due to the fact that the Nizam had a weak heart: the private apartments are on the ground floor while the reception rooms are relegated to the first floor. Access to these is via a monumental marble staircase lit by candelabras supported by sculptures and lined with portraits of the viceroys. The heavy brocade curtains, crystal chandeliers and Louis XVI furniture in one of the drawing-rooms conjure up the atmosphere of a European château in a Visconti film. There could be up to one hundred guests at the dining-room table, where the Nizam sat on a slightly raised armchair to compensate for his short stature. The dishes were made of gold and English musicians played to entertain the visitors. The smooth running of the palace was ensured by five hundred servants, while visits by distinguished guests provided an opportunity to carry out various innovations and improvements: showers of scented water in the bath-tubs when George V came to stay, and the renovation of the electrical system for the visit of the Prince of Wales in 1922.

The seventh Nizam, Mir Osman Ali Khan, in keeping with the superstitions associated with the palace, refused to make Falaknuma Palace his residence, keeping it, somewhat ironically, for passing guests. However, he did add the Jubilee Pavilion to the original building to display the gifts he had received at the Delhi Durbar of 1911. When he died the palace was virtually abandoned, emerging just once when all the lights were put on and it was flooded with music for the coronation of the eighth Nizam, Mir Barkat Ali Khan.

Like their legendary collections of jewels, the many magnificent palaces built in Hyderabad by the nizams bear witness to the power they exercised over their state - the largest and most populous in the Indian subcontinent. For instance, in the 1750s Nawab Salabath Jung built a palace complex known as Chauwmohalla in the heart of the old town. Near the Charminar, a triumphal arch erected in 1591 to celebrate the end of a plague epidemic, this complex was used as a private residence and administrative offices. A series of courts leads to four pavilions surrounding a quadrangle with a pool in the centre. The pavilions, the Mehtab Mahal (Palace of the Moon), Tah Niat Mahal, Aftab Mahal (Palace of the Sun) and Afzal Mahal, are reminiscent of residences on the Italian Riviera.

King Kothi Palace: the façade of the palace built by the seventh Nizam of Hyderabad.

Purani Haveli Palace: veranda.

Falaknuma Palace. Above and below: *day and night views*.

Above and below: *two terraces at Falaknuma Palace, one overlooking the onion turrets of the zenana, the other the surrounding countryside.*

Falaknuma Palace. Above: *ceiling fresco in the entrance hall.* Below: *neo-rococo style marble and stucco entrance hall. The walls are decorated with frescoes depicting European landscapes.* Opposite: *grand staircase with marble balustrade and sculptures supporting candelabra. On the walls, photograph portraits of viceroys of India.*

Falaknuma Palace. Above left: *clock made by Cooke & Kelvey with automata appearing when the hour strikes.*
Above right: *dressing-table in one of the bedrooms.* Below left: *detail of one of the many display cabinets in one of the first-floor state drawing-rooms.*
Below right: *in the same room a sofa with a porcelain panel above painted with oriental motifs.*

Falaknuma Palace. Opposite: *one of the first-floor state drawing-rooms; this one has no doors, opening directly off the gallery.*
Overleaf: *another state drawing-room, embellished with chinoiserie-style display cabinets arranged down the middle of the room and along the walls.*

Falaknuma Palace. Above: *first-floor games room*. Below: *English billiard table made by Burroughs & Watts*.

Falaknuma Palace: *First-floor gallery.*

Chauwmohalla Palace: the palace consists of four pavilions around a central pool.
Above: *balustrade of the Afzal Mahal pavilion, the ironwork inset with engraved glass plaques
reproducing verses from the Koran. Beyond, the Tah Niat Mahal pavilion.*
Opposite: *the covered entrance of the Afzal Mahal pavilion.*

Chauwmohalla Palace, the Afzal Mahal pavilion. Above: *balustrade around the gallery overlooking the drawing-room. The ironwork is inset with engraved glass medallions reproducing verses from the Koran.* Below and opposite: *views of the drawing-room.*

Purani Haveli. Above: *façade of the palace built in the eighteenth century.*
Opposite: *gallery with clothes cupboards. Each cupboard held the clothes for one day as the Nizam never wore the same garment twice.*

Glossary

BAGH:	*garden.*
BEGUM:	*Moslem princess.*
CHATTRI:	*kiosk or open pavilion with a cupola on top; ornamental or associated with funerals.*
DURBAR:	*audience held by the maharajas with their main courtiers and advisors in attendance.*
DURBAR HALL:	*ceremonial room in which Durbars were held.*
IMAMBARA:	*Moslem building or enclosure for ceremonies associated with Muharram.*
JAALI:	*openwork stone screen.*
JAMI MASJID:	*'Friday Mosque' where ritual Friday prayers are held.*
MAHAL:	*palace.*
MAHARAJA:	*Sanskrit word meaning 'Great King'. It was applied to all Indian princes, their importance being measured by the number of salvoes fired in the gun salute that greeted their appearance. These salutes, determined by Queen Victoria, were always fired in odd numbers, ranging from nine to twenty-one. Five princes were entitled to a 21-gun salute: the Maharajas of Mysore, Kashmir, Baroda and Gwalior and the Nizam of Hyderabad.*
MAHARANEE:	*wife of a maharaja.*
MASJID:	*mosque.*
MUHARRAM:	*Shiite religious festival and period of fasting.*
NAWAB:	*Moslem prince.*
NIZAM:	*Moslem title corresponding to the title maharaja. Only one royal family, the royal family of Hyderabad, was entitled to use it.*
PURDAH:	*word meaning 'curtain', used to describe the seclusion of women in the zenana. It was one of the few institutions preserved by Indian society after the collapse of the Mogul empire. An institution regarded as a sign of material wealth and distinction.*
RAJA:	*Indian prince; a less important title than maharaja.*
ZENANA:	*apartments in a palace or residence where women of high rank were kept in seclusion. It was completely forbidden for men to enter them.*

Bibliography

ALLEN, Charles and DWIVEDI, Sharada, *Lives of the Indian Princes,* London, 1984.

BARODA, Maharaja of, *The Palaces of India,* London, 1980.

BIRDWOOD, G., *The Industrial Arts of India,* London, 1880.

COLOGNI, Franco and NUSSBAUM, Eric, *Cartier, le joaillier du platine,* Paris, 1995.

DANIÉLOU, Alain, *Histoire de l'Inde,* Paris, 1971.

DEVI, Gayatri, *A Princess Remembers,* London and New York, 1985.

FITZROY, Yvonne, *Courts and Camps in India,* London, 1926.

FORBES, Rosita, *India of the Princes,* London, 1939.

GOLISH, Vitold de, *Splendeur et crépuscule des maharajahs,* Paris, 1963.

GOLISH, Vitold de, *L'Inde impudique des maharajahs,* Paris, 1973.

GOLISH, Vitold de, *L'Inde des paradis perdus,* Paris, 1990.

IRVING, Robert Grant, *Indian Summer, Lutyens, Baker and Imperial Delhi,* New Haven and London, 1981.

IVORY, James, *Autobiography of a Princess,* London, 1975.

KING, Peter, *The Shooting Field with Holland and Holland,* London, 1990.

LAPIERRE, Dominique and COLLINS, Larry, *Freedom at Midnight,* London, 1975

LEAR, Edward, *Indian Journal,* (edited by Ray Murphy), London, 1953.

LOSTY, J.P., *Calcutta, City of Palaces,* London, 1990.

MICHELL, George and MARTINELLI, Antonio, *Royal Palaces of India,* London, 1994.

MORROW, Ann, *Highness, the Maharajahs of India,* London, 1986.

NADELHOFFER, Hans, *Cartier,* Paris, 1984.

NÉRET, Gilles, *Boucheron, Histoire d'une dynastie de joailliers,* Paris, 1988.

NOU, Jean-Louis and POUCHEPADASS, Jacques, *Les Derniers Maharajahs,* Paris, 1980.

OKADA, Amina, *L'Inde du XIXe siècle: voyage aux sources de l'imaginaire,* Paris, 1991.

PATNAIK, Naveen, *A Second Paradise, Indian Courtly Life, 1590-1947,* London, 1985.

PATNAIK, Naveen, *A Desert Kingdom, the Rajputs of Bikaner,* London and New York, 1990.

ROBINSON, Andrew, *Maharaja,* Paris, 1988.

ROUSSELET, Louis, *L'Inde des rajahs, voyage dans l'Inde centrale et dans les présidences de Bombay et du Bengale,* Paris, 1875.

SUGICH, Michael, *Palaces of India, London,* 1992.

TADGELL, Christopher, *The History of Architecture in India from the Dawn of Civilization to the End of the Raj,* London, 1990.

TILLOTSON, G.H.R., *The Tradition of Indian Architecture,* New Haven and London, 1989.

Books with a number of contributors

Architecture in Victorian and Edwardian India, Bombay, 1994.

Arts of India 1550-1900, London, 1990.

Calcutta, the Living City, The Past, vol. 1, Oxford, 1990.

Histoire de l'Inde moderne (1480-1950), edited by Claude Markovits, Paris, 1994.

Magazine articles

DESCHARNES, Robert, 'En Inde, un palais 1930', *Connaissance des arts,* September 1970, no. 223.

'Christofle et les arts décoratifs', *Dossier de l'art,* July-August 1991.

MUTHESIUS, Eckart, 'The Architect and the Dancer', *The India Magazine,* January 1986

MUTHESIUS, Eckart, 'His Highness and the Bauhaus Architect', *The India Magazine,* March 1986.

WILSON, Henry, 'The Boras of Siddhpur', *The World of Interiors,* April 1994.

Acknowledgements

First and foremost we would like to thank Cristalleries Baccarat, their chairwoman, Mme. Anne-Claire Taittinger, Fabienne de Sèze and Pascal Andriveau for giving us the opportunity to complete this project. The journeys to India and within the subcontinent that made this book possible were effected thanks to Air India, the director of its Paris agency, Mr. Bakhshi, Mme. Nicole Bénard of its public relations department, and the Indian Tourist Office in Paris and Delhi. Thanks are also due to KLM Airlines, M. Théo Pielage and Mme. Evelyne Quesnot. Our special thanks are due to Mr. Oberoi, owner of the international chain of Oberoi hotels, to Mr. Sony Iqbal, the company's European marketing director, Mrs. Indira Banerji, the public relations director of the Oberoi chain, and all the managers of the various Oberoi hotels for their superb hospitality. We are also extremely grateful to Kodak, Ilford and Polaroid for their support in providing materials and at the Publimond Photo laboratory.

In India we would like to thank the following people for their warm welcome and support: the Kapurthala family, in particular H.H. Sukjit Singh, Maharaja of Kapurthala, H.H. the Rajmata Suchila Kumari and her daughter Princess Rajyashree of Bikaner, H.H. Madhaurao Scindia, Maharaja of Gwalior, Ratanjit Singh of Simla, the Patiala family, Dr. Karan Singh, Maharaja of Jammu and Kashmir, H.H. the Maharaja of Baroda and his wife, Shri Gaj Singh II, Maharaja of Jodhpur and Princess Baiji of Jodhpur, and H.H. the Maharaja of Jaipur.

We would also like to thank H.H. Vasundara Raje, Maharanee of Dholpur and her son Dushyant, the Begum of Rampur, her daughter-in-law Begum Yaseen and her son, Nawab Syed Mohammad Kazim Ali Khan, the Nawab of Pataudi and his wife Begum Sharmila Tagore, H.H. Raj Sahib Pratap Sinh, Maharaja of Wankaner and his son Digvijay Sinh, Princesses Mira, Purna and Uma of Morvi, H.H. the Maharaja of Limbdi and his wife Snemlata Kumari, H.H. Srikanta Datta Narasi, Maharaja of Mysore; in Hyderabad, H.H. the Nizam, M. Javeri, Air Chief Marshall Idris Latif and his wife Begum Bilkees and Lakshmi Devi Raj; Roy Macchia, a planter from Coorg, Ahmed Saith and his six brothers at Ootacamund; in Delhi, Francis Wacziarg, Rina Singh, Hershad Kumari Sharma of Intach, the poet Momin Latif, the architect Raj Rewal and his wife Hélène, Carmenza Jaramillo, the Ambassadress of Colombia, Isabelle Elkhadi of the Spanish Embassy, and Mrs. Adarsh Gill; in Bombay, Umaima Mulla-Feroze, the painter Jehangir Sabavala and his wife Shareen, Jerry Mangoo, Pranlal Bhogilal and Rashmi Poddar; in Calcutta, Lady Muckerjee, Raja Mrigendro Mullick of the Marble Palace, the Mullick family, Raja Adhish Chandra Sinha and his wife Mary, Bimla Poddar, Jayant Hirjee, Aveek Sarkar, editor of the Telegraph *and his wife Rakhi, Sandip Ray, Rusi Modi, Chairman of Air India, Rita Sen, Ruby Pal Choudhuri, chairwoman of the Alliance française and the journalist Jaya Chaliha.*

Also in India, our heartfelt thanks are due to His Excellency M. Philippe Petit, France's ambassador in Delhi, and his wife; to Mme. Luce Rudent of the Service culturel in Delhi and to other French residents in India, from Ahmedabad to Calcutta. In France we would like to thank the Association française d'Action artistique within the Ministry for Foreign Affairs who awarded Anne Garde the Villa-Médicis-Hors-les-Murs bursary to complete this project.

For their help in establishing valuable contacts between France and India, all thanks are due to His Excellency Mr. Ranjit Sethi, India's ambassador in France, and to Mrs. Veena Sikri, Minister for Franco-Indian Economic Relations. Finally we would like to acknowledge the advice and sustained support for our project shown by Mme. Krishna Riboud, M. Jean-Louis Dumas-Hermès, M. and Mme. Guy de Valence, Mme. Amina Okada, curator of the Musée Guimet, Mr Martin Meade, architectural historian, Mme. Francine Boura of the Monde de l'Inde et de l'Asie, the Prats family from the château Cos d'Estournel, and Pierre Lawton in Bordeaux.

We would also like to express our gratitude to the following people for their valuable assistance: Mme. Dominique Biard, M. Cosme Carpentier de Gourdon, Mme. Lydia Fasoli, M. Jean-Louis Gaillemin, Mme. Marie-Noëlle des Horts, M. Aurélien Moline, M. Jean-Luc Olivié, curator of the Centre National du Verre at the Musée des Arts décoratifs, M. Alexandre Pradère, Mme. Tamara Préaud, director of the archives of the Manufacture nationale de céramique de Sèvres, M. Guillaume Prieur, Mme. Dany Sautot and Mme. Pascaline Pascal at Baccarat, Mme. Nadia Tazi; and to the following companies for their collaboration: the Boucheron company, M. Michel Aliaga and Mme. Betty Jais at Cartier, Christofle, Galerie Doria, M. Alain Drach at Holland & Holland, and Maples.